YO-BSF-645

FREE-TRADE FEDERALISM: NEGOTIATING THE CANADIAN AGREEMENT ON INTERNAL TRADE

The pressures of regional as well as global free trade are crossing ever more deeply into the fabric of Canadian federalism. Based on interviews with key negotiators, and acknowledging the entwined histories of trade policy, industrial and regional policy, and federal–provincial policy, Doern and MacDonald provide an integrated account of the negotiations that in 1993–4 led to the Agreement on Internal Trade (AIT) among the federal government, the provinces, and both territorial governments. The authors examine both the central negotiations and the trade-offs made by the federal government, key clusters of provinces, and sectoral representatives in fields such as investment, regional policy, procurement, the environment, and resources. Arguing that AIT and FTA/NAFTA should be seen as the fourth and fifth pillars of Canada's bedrock institutions – joining the parliamentary system, federalism, and the Charter of Rights and Freedoms – the authors position AIT as a significant achievement, signalling important changes in both federalism and policy formation. They argue that, as the AIT is built upon, key issues regarding Canada's social union that have yet to be confronted will increasingly arise.

BRUCE DOERN is a professor in the School of Public Administration at Carleton University, and joint chair in Public Policy in the Department of Politics at Exeter University. He is presently actively involved in the Carleton Research Unit on Innovation, Science and Environment (CRUISE).

MARK R. MACDONALD is nearing completion of his doctoral thesis for a PhD in public policy at the School of Public Administration, Carleton University, where he is also a sessional lecturer.

G. BRUCE DOERN AND MARK MACDONALD

Free-Trade Federalism: Negotiating the Canadian Agreement on Internal Trade

UNIVERSITY OF TORONTO PRESS
Toronto Buffalo London

© University of Toronto Press Incorporated 1999
Toronto Buffalo London
Printed in Canada

ISBN 0-8020-4223-6 (cloth)
ISBN 0-8020-8072-3 (paper)

Printed on acid-free paper

Canadian Cataloguing in Publication Data

Doern, G. Bruce, 1942–
    Free trade federalism

    Includes bibliographical references and index.
    ISBN 0-8020-4223-6 (bound)
    ISBN 0-8020-8072-3 (pbk.)

    1. Interprovincial commerce – Canada.*   2. Interprovincial relations –
Canada.*   3. Trade regulation – Canada – Provinces.   4. Nontariff trade
barriers – Canada – Provinces.   I. MacDonald, Mark, 1967–   . II. Title.

HF3226.5.D63 1999   381′.5′0971   C98-932083-9

University of Toronto Press acknowledges the financial assistance to its
publishing program of the Canada Council for the Arts and the Ontario
Arts Council.

For Joan
and
Nancy

AUGUSTANA UNIVERSITY COLLEGE
LIBRARY

Contents

PREFACE   xi

ABBREVIATIONS   xiii

1 **Introduction**   3
Free Trade and Federalism: Key Concepts and Issues   4
The Agreement in Brief   9
Structure and Organization of This Book   13

PART ONE: FRAMEWORK, CONTEXT, AND HISTORY

2 **The Evolution of Three Policy Fields: A Framework for 1990s Free-Trade Federalism**   17
Regional-Industrial Policy   18
Trade Policy   21
Federal–Provincial Policy   26
The Social Union: The Missing Dimension?   32
Conclusions   35

3 **Getting on the Agenda: Key Stages in the Internal Trade Policy and Negotiation Process**   37
The Road to the Negotiations   38
Key Negotiation Stages   48
The Institutions in Action   53
Conclusions   56

PART TWO: THE NEGOTIATIONS AND MULTIPLE–POLICY
FIELD POLICY MAKING

4 **The Core of the Agreement: The Provinces and Negotiation
Issues and Dynamics** 59
Alberta and Manitoba as Pro-Free-Trade Allies 60
Quebec and the Political Need for an Economic Union 63
The NDP Provinces: Variously Sceptical Free-Trade Critics 66
Atlantic Canada and the Territories: Fearing Abandonment while
   Pursuing More Open Markets 73
Arthur Mauro and the Internal Trade Secretariat 78
Conclusions 81

5 **Sectoral Negotiations I: Procurement and Regional
Policy** 83
Procurement 85
Regional Economic Policies: The Presence at Every Table 93
Conclusions 96

6 **Sectoral Negotiations II: Investment, Labour Mobility, and
Environment** 98
Investment 99
Labour Mobility 104
Environmental Protection 110
Conclusions 116

7 **Sectoral Negotiations III: The Agricultural and Food Goods,
Resource-Processing, and Energy Sectors** 119
Agricultural and Food Goods 121
Natural Resources Processing 127
Energy as the Missing Chapter 130
Conclusions 132

8 **'Rules about Rules,' Dispute Resolution, and Institutions** 134
Rules about Rules? Standards and Regulatory Measures as a
   Horizontal Issue 134
The Key Provisions on Dispute Resolution and Institutions 137
The Negotiating Dynamics and Issues: A Closer Look 140
The United Parcel Service Case and the Dispute-Resolution
   Process 142

Dispute Resolution and Debates about the Federal Trade-and-Commerce Power   146
Conclusions   149

9 Conclusions   151
Analytical Summary: The AIT Process in General   154
Institutions and Multi–Policy Field Negotiations   158
Dispute Resolution, the Trade-and-Commerce Power, and 'Rules about Rules'   161
Future Free-Trade Federalism: The AIT, Quebec, and the Social Union   163

REFERENCES   169
INDEX   183

Preface

The primary sources on which this book is based are the published literature and government documents cited. Interestingly, few formal published policy or strategy statements were issued by the provinces on the Agreement on Internal Trade. However, we did have access to a considerable body of correspondence between levels of government and between negotiating tables and the main table. These documents cannot be cited because they are recent in nature and because a subsequent round of negotiations was expected as we conducted our work, but they did assist us in obtaining a better sense of the process.

The fifty interviews we conducted in late 1995, 1996, and early 1997, largely with federal and provincial officials involved in the negotiations, as well as with some individuals from the private sector, are also an important source for this book. The interviews were granted on an undertaking from us that no expressed views would be attributed to individuals. This confidentiality provision was important as it allowed us to obtain frank comments and opinions about the negotiation processes and issues. The purpose of this book is not to produce a 'smoking gun' account of who did what to whom in a complex trade negotiation and policy process. Rather, it is to supply an overall sense of the issues and interplay involved. Key officials in the federal government and in all ten provinces also read and commented on earlier drafts of the chapters on the general and sectoral negotiations.

This book could not have been researched and written at all without this mixture of public and interview-based sources and the approach set out above. The final product must be assessed against the logic, carefulness of argument, and overall persuasiveness brought to the subject and events by the authors. But different interpretations undoubtedly accompany any complex event and set of decision processes. In light of the nature of these sources and approaches, this book must be seen as only a partial or initial history of the internal-trade negotiations of 1993–4. A more complete history would need to be based on federal and provincial Cabinet and other information, to which the authors were not privy. Nonetheless, an initial interpretation and account is useful. The existing small stock of literature on the Agreement on Internal Trade itself is primarily a critique of the agreement rather than an account of how the deal was done or of the broader political economy of free-trade federalism. Our study complements this literature, with an examination of the negotiation process, the institutions involved, and the broader implications for Canadian federalism.

Special thanks are due to all those persons who cooperated through interviews and to officials in the Internal Trade Group at Industry Canada. We are especially indebted to Bob Knox, whose initial encouragement got the research started and whose own efforts helped keep internal trade on the national agenda. Two anonymous reviewers selected by the publisher also offered extremely helpful comments. All of those mentioned have made this a better book. We are responsible for any remaining weaknesses or errors in the analysis.

Last but certainly not least, we gratefully acknowledge the funding support for our research which came from the Social Science and Humanities Research Council of Canada, Industry Canada, the School of Public Administration at Carleton University, and the Politics Department, University of Exeter.

Bruce Doern and Mark MacDonald
January 1998

Abbreviations

AIT	Agreement on Internal Trade
CCME	Canadian Council of Ministers of Environment
CIDA	Canadian International Development Agency
CMIT	Committee of Ministers of Internal Trade
CREDM	Committee of Regional Economic Development Ministers
DFAIT	Department of Foreign Affairs and International Trade
DREE	Department of Regional Economic Expansion
DRIE	Department of Regional and Industrial Expansion
EC	European Community
ENGO	environmental non-governmental organization
EU	European Union
FIRA	Foreign Investment Review Agency
FLMM	Forum of Labour Market Ministers
FPATPC	Federal–Provincial Agricultural Trade Policy Committee
FTA	Free Trade Agreement (between Canada and the United States)
GATT	General Agreement on Tariffs and Trade
HRDC	Human Resources and Development Canada
IRBP	Industrial and Regional Benefits Program
ISTC	Industry, Science and Technology Canada
ITS	Internal Trade Secretariat
MASH	municipalities, academic institutions, and social-service and health entities (the MASH sector)
NAFTA	North American Free Trade Agreement (between Canada, the United States, and Mexico)
NDP	New Democratic Party
NRCan	Natural Resources Canada

OECD	Organization for Economic Cooperation and Development
PQ	Parti Québécois
SAGIT	Sectoral Advisory Group on International Trade
TCS	Trade Commissioner Service
UPS	United Parcel Service
WTO	World Trade Organization

FREE-TRADE FEDERALISM:
NEGOTIATING THE CANADIAN AGREEMENT ON
INTERNAL TRADE

1

Introduction

The term 'free-trade federalism' will strike some as embodying the consummate odd couple of Canadian political-economic analysis. 'Free trade' evokes a world of global trade among countries, whereas 'federalism' suggests a domestic governing system whereby powers to make laws are divided between levels of national and provincial government. The former is quintessentially about economics, and the latter is unambiguously political in its focus. However odd the couple may seem to be, paired they have always been. Free-trade federalism is both an old and a new subject.

It is a subject of historical importance because, when federations such as those of the United States and Canada were formed, the rationale for creating a federal political structure was centred, in part, on establishing an internal common market or economic union. Free trade within such a union tended to be seen as the free flow of goods and the absence of tariffs. The absence of tariffs was all the more significant in these earlier historical periods because the tariff was the main source of revenue for the state. Free-trade federalism is also a subject of new or refurbished importance, in the last decade in particular, because of global and national developments that range from the impacts of free- or liberalized-trade agreements such as the FTA, NAFTA, and the GATT–WTO Uruguay Round Agreement, to the internal stresses of possible Quebec separation, which is predicated upon promises of political sovereignty coupled with free trade with Canada. Europe, too, has vigorously pursued the establishment of an integrated internal market while only indirectly and inadequately facing up to the establishment of an explicit federal system of governing. Indeed, Quebec sovereigntists and some Quebec federalists have seen the European model as the solution for Canada (Liberal Party of Quebec 1991).

If free-trade federalism is both an old and a new subject, it is ultimately also a very big subject. This book examines only some aspects of it, namely, those centred on the context for, and dynamics of, negotiating the 1993–4 Agreement on Internal Trade (AIT). More particularly, the book has a fourfold purpose: first, to examine the main issues and contours of free-trade federalism in Canada; second, to provide an account of the broad negotiation processes in 1993–4 that produced the internal-trade agreement between the federal government and the provinces and territorial governments; third, to provide an initial assessment of the processes and institutions involved and prospects for their future adaptation in Canadian free-trade federalism; and, fourth, to assess the broader institutional aspects of policy making through larger-scale international trade-like negotiations in the realm of federal–provincial relations.

The complex eighteen-chapter AIT is in many ways a significant agreement, but it was achieved in a remarkably non-public way and with limited attention from Canadian voters (Trebilcock and Schwanen 1995). Had federal and provincial representatives been directly negotiating changes to such matters as the constitution, federal–provincial tax agreements, or budgets and deficit reductions, the glare of publicity would have been considerable. In many ways, the AIT is as important as any other aspect of Canadian federalism and the Canadian economy but is seen as technical, and even arcane – hence, its negotiation out of the limelight. This does not mean that there was no public attention paid to the negotiations and issues involved, but the AIT was not a central concern of the average voter or, arguably, even of most interest groups.

The Agreement on Internal Trade, however, is in fact an extremely important development in the context of both trade policy and federal–provincial relations. In the first part of this brief introduction, we set out some basic issues that are at the heart of free trade, on the one hand, and federalism, on the other. We also sketch out in a preliminary way the key political-economic features that are central to any overall account and assessment of the agreement and its institutions as a manifestation of free-trade federalism. We then provide an initial profile of the basic features of the AIT, focusing only on its broad architecture and core provisions. More detailed provisions are examined in later chapters. Finally, we outline the basic organization of this book.

Free Trade and Federalism: Key Concepts and Issues

The literature on free trade and on federalism is voluminous and complex, but it is helpful to begin with a quite basic view of the two concepts and then to move to an understanding of their subtleties and nuances as our analytical journey proceeds. Free trade as an economic concept is centred on the theory of comparative advantage (Krugman and Obstfeld 1994; Trebilcock and Howse 1995). Initially devised for the analysis of trade among nations, it argued and showed that the world would be better off if countries specialized in the production and exchange of goods in which they had a relative advantage over other countries. Though it focused on trade in goods, the theory implied the mobilization, in a similar vein, of all of the factors of production, including capital, labour, and knowledge or technology.

Free trade as an operating concept is usually seen in the context of intensive post–Second World War efforts to liberalize, or make 'freer,' international trade through successive rounds of negotiations under the General Agreement on Tariffs and Trade (GATT). As a laboratory for the application of free-trade theory, the GATT experiment has been conducted ultimately against the backdrop of a world seeking to avoid the destructive high-tariff protectionism of the 1930s (Hart 1993, 1994; Doern and Tomlin 1991a). While GATT agreements became ever more complex, their broad thrust was to continuously lower tariffs, ideally to the point where they would reach zero, and trade, in this sense, would be free. It would not, however, be free trade in the sense of the full and free mobility of all of the factors of production across national boundaries. Indeed, GATT's provisions to endorse 'free-trade agreements' among countries or regional groups of countries defined free trade in the narrower sense. These were to be free-trade areas and not common markets, where, in the latter case, in principle, there would be freedoms for labour mobility as well as for other factors of production.

Consider now some of the essentials of federalism (Watts 1989a; Simeon 1972). Federal constitutions vary considerably, but at their core they provide for a system of dual or shared sovereignty in the sense that lawmaking powers are divided on the basis of subject matter or some related basis between two levels of government – federal and state in the United States, federal and *Länder* in Germany; and, of course, federal and provincial in Canada. A common electorate ultimately elects both governments and holds them accountable, and a system of courts ensures the appropriate constitutionality of their laws, policies, and actions. Federalism as a system of government arises out of the core socio-economic circumstances of a given political and geographical territory in that factors such as ethnic and cultural diversity or inherent spatial size may create demands for such shared forms of governance. Such forces may also lead to the break-up or attempted break-up of federations.

Federalism in and of itself does not tell us how governments in total within a federation will actually govern or how far they will intervene in the marketplace or in social spheres. The nature and extent of governing have obviously changed over the decades as both the welfare state and the industrial-policy state expanded and waned. The division of powers between levels of government will, however, have some effect on what kind of internal common market is intended to exist in a federation. In early federations such as Canada, these were partially expressed in the assignment of powers over interprovincial trade and commerce (in goods) to the federal government. But powers of taxation and powers to impose tariffs also defined some of the contours of what was a full common market or economic union (Norrie, Simeon, and Krasnick 1986). Thus in strict terms Canada has, from the outset, understood free-trade federalism as more than the absence of tariffs.

Clearly, however, such basic notions do not take the controversy out of determining just 'how free' an internal intra-federalist state market is deemed to be as time goes on and as economies change. For example, the debate about the AIT was precipitated by a view that the Canadian internal market had too many barriers (read: excessively interventionist government policies, especially provincial policies) and therefore that it was not as free an internal market as that of the United States. Not only did the U.S. political system endorse capitalism, free markets, and limited government more enthusiastically, it also pursued more vigilant policies regarding the defence of interstate commerce and competition or anti-trust than Canada's did. Even the European Union (EU) was seen in some quarters as having a more open and fulsome economic union. This was a much more dubious argument than that arising from the U.S. comparison, but it emerged in part because the EU (earlier the European Community, or EC) was formally committed through its treaties to a defence of the 'four freedoms': the freedom of movement of goods, services, capital, and labour among the EU's member states (Williams 1991; Doern and Wilks 1996).

Such basic concepts of free trade and of federalism are crucial for understanding free-trade federalism and the AIT, but they are obviously not in themselves a sufficient framework for analysis. More layers of conceptual and practical reality have to be added as we proceed. In particular, four related and underlying political-economic features need to be briefly highlighted, features to which we return throughout this book.

These are: (a) the increased influence of international trade–policy players into both the industrial-regional and overall federal-provincial realms of policy making; (b) the extent to which the AIT is seen as an economic and trade agreement as distinct from a deal on quasi-constitutional governance in a democratic federation; (c) the relationship of federal and provincial goals and negotiating strategies to the underlying real economy of each province and/or region and to past notions of regional economic development and industrial policy; and (d) how the AIT was seen in terms of Canadian national unity.

The first feature derives from the fact that the AIT was a negotiation which brought together, in one macro, multi–policy field decision-making process, ministers and officials from three different traditions and policy communities: industrial-regional policy, trade policy, and federal–provincial relations. The basic nature of these conjoined realms and how each component adapted to the other are of central importance to the political analysis.

The question of mixing and melding players from the three groupings, however, goes well beyond the players themselves and their sense of the AIT process being a 'negotiation' compared with previous forms of policy making. It also embraces the overriding ideas and agendas that were involved. The economic origins of the 'internal trade' debate itself are traced in chapters 2 and 3, but what must be clearly highlighted here is the fact that the federal government saw the negotiations overwhelmingly as a natural extension of the previously entrenched free-trade agenda of the 1986–93 period (Internal Trade Secretariat 1994; Interim Secretariat 1992). Some provinces, such as Alberta and Manitoba, also supported this view strongly.

Other provinces, such as British Columbia and Saskatchewan, however, saw the main issues as comprising not only a trade agenda but also a federalism and governance agenda. Their main concerns centred on the powers of provincial governments, and what legitimate objectives were deemed to be crucial for governments in the 1990s and beyond (Lenihan 1995). In short, the provinces were facing the same questions in a domestic realm that the federal government had faced internationally in the FTA and NAFTA negotiations. This view has many manifestations, which the analysis undertaken in this book will bring out.

The third political-economic feature of free-trade federalism and of the negotiations is more conventional but nonetheless crucial. It is simply that each participant (whether a provincial or the federal government) saw its goals and negotiating tactics partially in terms of how it saw the underlying national and regional economy and its views of past regional economic-development policies. A 1996 Statistics Canada study brought out some key features of internal and overall trade. Atlantic, Central, and Western Canada traded extensively within their own respective regions. Only Ontario and Quebec registered an interprovincial-trade surplus, but both had sizeable international-trade deficits. British Columbia had by far the largest interprovincial-trade deficit but had an international-trade surplus that was second only to Alberta's. Services accounted for 40 per cent of interprovincial trade, with transportation and wholesale services accounting for one-fifth of all interprovincial trade (Statistics Canada 1996, 12–19).

Thus, provincial strategies were based, in part, on their patterns of trade. Ontario and Quebec's positions, for example, were couched in the full knowledge of their strong trade. British Columbia adopted a more combative approach in the negotiations, in part because it was not as dependent on trade with the rest of Canada and was focusing on its growing trade with the Pacific Rim (Schwanen 1995).

Some of the issues related to the underlying economy were also being debated from the perspective of historical regional and industrial economic policies, as practised in the previous three decades by both federal and provincial governments. We examine this perspective in chapter 2, but it was clear that the 'regional' paradigm and its various versions of addressing and reducing regional disparity were increasingly under attack from several sources of pressure and argument (Savoie 1986; McFetridge 1985; McGee 1992). Indeed, throughout their heyday, regional policies were always in tension with national economic-development policies, if the latter were thought of as being intended to maximize overall Canadian GNP.

The final part of the elemental calculus of negotiations for the federal government and the provinces was the immediate and longer-term issue of national unity. This was linked to the Meech Lake and Charlottetown constitutional failures (Cohen 1990; Simeon 1990; Cook 1994; McRoberts and Monahan 1993). But it was also tied to the immediate prospect of an expected late-1994 Quebec election. This produced a need for success, or, as federal negotiators frequently put it, 'Canada needs a win!' However, the Quebec situation also affected particular provisions in the agreement as each delegation reached its own judgment as to what it thought the Quebec Liberal Government might need to defend itself against the Parti Québécois sovereigntist Opposition. Delegations also had to assess how those same remaining provisions might be used by a

Parti Québécois government in power. During the negotiations, as the fall 1994 election loomed as a greater and greater certainty, the Quebec situation clearly supplied a further reason why the 30 June deadline for the AIT negotiations could not be allowed to slip.

There were also other ways in which national unity entered the politics of the negotiation and the values behind it. This was that free internal trade was itself advocated, especially by the federal government, on the principled premise that individual Canadians, as citizens, workers, investors, and business persons, should have the right to work and invest anywhere in Canada. This, it was argued, would foster a greater sense of national unity at an individual level (Cohen 1995; Trebilcock and Behboodi 1995).

Each of the elements discussed above is an important apsect of the negotiations as they evolved. These elements also represent the multiple criteria for assessment which many applied both during and after the negotiations. Before going further, however, we need to know more about the Agreement on Internal Trade itself.

The Agreement in Brief

The basic architecture of the agreement must be appreciated to make sense of the account of the negotiations presented in chapters 4 to 8 of this book. Table 1, which identifies the six parts and eighteen chapters of the agreement, is instructive in this regard. Each part is introduced briefly here, with more texture provided in subsequent chapters.

The most basic point about the agreement is that the bulk of its terms are in Part IV, which comprises the eleven chapters dealing with specific rules. These were handled mainly by the sectoral negotiating teams or tables, although the procurement provisions were also kept very close to the main table of negotiators (see chapter 3), who oversaw the entire package. A point worth noting as well is that the 'sector' chapters and tables were in fact not typically sectors, in the sense of vertical industrial sectors such as producing autos or steel. Some fit this category, such as the chapters on alcoholic beverages, and agricultural and food goods, but many other so-called sectors were in fact aspects of internal trade that were horizontal, and hence cut across all or most sectors of the economy. This was certainly true of procurement, investment, labour mobility, consumer-related measures and standards, and environmental protection. Other chapters such as communications, transportation, natural-resources processing, and energy were more hybrid in nature. They were

TABLE 1
The Agreement on Internal Trade at a Glance
(Six Parts and Eighteen Chapters)

Preamble

PART I – GENERAL
Chapter 1   Operating Principles
Chapter 2   General Definitions

PART II – CONSTITUTIONAL AUTHORITIES
Chapter 3   Reaffirmation of Constitutional Powers and Responsibilities

PART III – GENERAL RULES
Chapter 4   General Rules

PART IV – SPECIFIC RULES
Chapter 5   Procurement
Chapter 6   Investment
Chapter 7   Labour Mobility
Chapter 8   Consumer-Related Measures and Standards
Chapter 9   Agricultural and Food Goods
Chapter 10   Alcoholic Beverages
Chapter 11   Natural Resources Processing
Chapter 12   Energy
Chapter 13   Communications
Chapter 14   Transportation
Chapter 15   Environmental Protection

PART V – INSTITUTIONAL PROVISIONS AND DISPUTE RESOLUTION PROCEDURES
Chapter 16   Institutional Provisions
Chapter 17   Dispute Resolution Procedures

PART VI – FINAL PROVISIONS
Chapter 18   Final Provisions
Annexes

---

certainly seen as industrial sectors, but they were also horizontal and economy-wide in nature, in that they were clearly a crucial aspect of production in virtually every other sector of the economy.

The division between general and specific rules is crucial. Ideally, in any trade agreement the general rules ought to be paramount, with specific rules flowing from them and not contradicting them. No agreement is perfect in this respect, and the AIT certainly flouts this structure in many ways. Indeed, the essence of the negotiations was, in many respects, the issue of which chapters would take precedence over other chapters.

The preamble and the provisions in Parts I, II, and III set out the basic objectives, operating principles, and general rules. We analyse these in chapters 3 and 4, but, at its core, the purpose of the agreement was stated to be the promotion of 'an open, efficient and stable domestic market for long-term job creation, economic growth and stability' and, accordingly, 'to reduce and eliminate to the extent possible, barriers to the free movement of persons, goods, services and investments within Canada.' The agreement was also intended to 'promote equal economic opportunity for Canadians' and several related objectives regarding competitiveness, sustainable environmental development, and better consultation on internal-trade matters.

The preamble also reaffirms that nothing in the agreement alters the legislative or other authority of Parliament or the legislatures of the provinces under the Constitution of Canada. The agreement, in short, was not an exercise in constitutional change. This point was crucial in both the legal and the political context of the agreement, though it remains problematic in terms of whether the AIT is, in a certain way, a kind of 'side deal' on the constitution (Swinton 1995a, 1995b). This point is discussed in chapter 9 of this book.

The 'general rules' provisions in Part III of the agreement include those regarding reciprocal non-discrimination, right of entry and exit, and transparency, but they also include provisions regarding 'legitimate objectives.' These provisions were insisted upon by the provinces so as to enable them to practise policies that were legitimate even though they might be contrary to some or all of the general rules (Lenihan 1995). Such practises carried out in the name of 'legitimate objectives' would still have to be put in place in such a way that they did not 'impair unduly' the access of economic players, nor could they be 'more trade restrictive than necessary.'

Part IV contains the specific rules of the sectors and areas noted above. Procurement is by far the largest chapter, reflecting its particular sensitivity in the negotiation. It deals, of course, with the government's own purchases of goods and services and with the extent to which a province could discriminate in favour of its own citizens and firms in its decisions to purchase items with its taxpayers' money. The shortest 'chapter' is on energy, which is in fact a one-line entry, since no agreement was reached. As we will see in chapter 7 of this book, this failure to agree resulted in large part from disputes over the transmission, or 'wheeling,' of electricity across provincial boundaries.

The other sectoral chapters (eight of which we examine) all begin with statements regarding the extent to which their provisions are an exception to (in whole or part) or governed by the general rules. With regard to both their content and their negotiating processes, these sectors should be seen in two important contexts. First, these chapters were typically negotiated by officials from the other line departments of the governments involved. Second, many of the issues and policy problems they were dealing with had been on their sectoral agendas for years. Accordingly, one of the issues in the analysis as a whole is whether the internal-trade arena of decision making simply continued the process without much change, or whether it altered the dynamics precisely because it was a different political-economic arena for such decisions. Chapter 9 comments on these themes after eight of the sectors have been examined in Part 2 of this book.

Parts V and VI of the agreement deal with institutional provisions and dispute resolution, and so-called final provisions. These issues were very much in the hands of the main table of chief negotiators, and ultimately those of the internal trade ministers as well. The final provisions included politically crucial issues which secured varying kinds of full or partial exemption from the agreement, including regional economic development, aboriginal peoples, culture, national security, taxation, and the financial sector. Many of these were included at the behest of the federal government, and relate to its policy spheres rather than just provincial ones.

The institutional provisions in chapter 16 of the agreement establish a basis for implementing and building on the deal. A Committee on Internal Trade is established, composed of Cabinet-level representation. A jointly funded Internal Trade Secretariat is also established (now based in Winnipeg). Also established is a Working Party on Adjustment to assess the effects of the agreement on each province in each fiscal year. This provision was insisted upon by Saskatchewan and the Atlantic provinces to provide a mechanism to examine, and therefore, it is hoped, deal with some of the expected adverse effects that the agreement might have in some sectors and regions.

Even more crucial, however, are the agreed-upon provisions regarding dispute-resolution procedures, many of which are modelled on international-trade dispute-settlement practises (Howse 1995a; Swinton 1995b). These cover more than twenty pages of the agreement and, as chapters 4 and 8 show, were the subject of considerable controversy. There are procedures for both government-to-government and person-to-government dispute resolution. It was the latter provisions for private access, and how extensive to make such access, that led to the most vigorous debate. The essence of both types of dispute resolution is to force parties into each chapter's dispute-resolution processes. Only after these sectoral routes have been exhausted can the AIT's overall processes be used. In both of these arenas, the approach is to enable a sequence of steps to occur, beginning with consultations, then a possible request for assistance, and finally a request for a panel, and a panel stage. If a dispute goes to the ultimate AIT-wide panel stage, then implementation of the independent panel report will first rely on compliance by the parties or perhaps the influence of adverse publicity. Under prescribed circumstances, retaliatory action can be taken.

The private-access procedures contain a screening process to eliminate frivolous complaints that precedes the steps outlined above. An important exception is that a panel report may contain an award of costs related to proceedings but not for damages. Dispute-avoidance and -settlement steps also vary somewhat in some of the sectoral chapters.

Structure and Organization of This Book

The next seven chapters of this book are divided into two parts, the first dealing with the framework and historical context, and the second with the core negotiations and the sectoral negotiation tables and arenas. Chapter 2 thus presents a framework and longer-term, historical policy context for the analysis, centred on the evolution of three policy fields whose key features and historical trajectories are significant: regional-industrial policy, international-trade policy, and overall federal–provincial policy. It also brings in the issue of Canada as a social union, a debate that was not of primary importance to the AIT processes but which has emerged since in reactions to both international and domestic free trade. Chapter 3 deals more specifically with how the internal-trade issue got on the agenda in roughly the last decade, and profiles the main players and early stages of the negotiations. Federal government objectives are also examined in more detail in the context of this winding, decade-long road to the negotiations.

In Part Two of this book, the negotiation process is examined at the macro and micro levels. Chapter 4 looks at the macro dynamics of the negotiations. It deals mainly with the positions and stances of the provinces and of the Internal Trade Secretariat, and also with the role of the neutral chair of the main negotiating table, Arthur Mauro. But the positions and role of the federal government are also examined in more depth. The basic stances of all governments centred around key provisions on general versus specific rules, legitimate objectives, regional development, procurement, and dispute settlement.

Chapters 5–8 examine a total of eight selected sectoral chapter negotiations. The clusters or groupings of sectors in each chapter are based on a mixture of rationales. In part, they are grouped simply because, in the negotiation process itself, the sectors were closely linked and, in some real sense, were in tension. Thus, procurement is examined in chapter 5 along with the closely related overall concerns about regional policy. In other respects, the clusters reflect areas that have some common kinds of trade or policy characteristics. For example, chapter 6 focuses on investment, labour mobility, and environment, each of which deals with horizontal or framework rules for the economy as a whole. In chapter 7, attention turns to three natural resource–centred sectors: agricultural and food goods; natural-resources processing (in forestry, mining, and the fisheries); and energy. These are sectors that raise major issues about provincial ownership and control of renewable and non-renewable resources, but where aspects of federal jurisdiction are also central. The treatment in each of these three sectoral chapters is necessarily brief but is intended to give some of the flavour of the key issues and of the outcomes entrenched in the agreement, set against a basic look at recent policy history.

Chapter 8 provides an account of the negotiations on dispute resolution and on institutions, including the role of the agreement as a regulatory instrument and one involving standard-setting. The analysis is also linked to the debate about the federal 'trade and commerce' power under the constitution and includes an initial look at one of the early disputes, the United Parcel Service (UPS) controversy. The case brought by British Columbia challenged New Brunswick's actions in successfully attracting UPS to consolidate customer-service operations from locations in three provinces.

In chapter 9, conclusions are offered regarding the overall nature and implications of free-trade federalism and of the negotiation processes and issues likely to influence the adaptation of the AIT and its institutions. We also look at possible implications of the Quebec issue and of the emerging, more explicit discussion of Canada as a social as well as an economic union.

PART ONE:
FRAMEWORK, CONTEXT, AND HISTORY

2

The Evolution of Three Policy Fields: A Framework for 1990s Free-Trade Federalism

To provide a framework and larger historical context for 1990s free-trade federalism, we need to trace the basic evolution of three policy fields, or realms, and the manner in which they converged and collided in the 1990s in general, and in the Agreement on Internal Trade's macro multi–policy field negotiation in particular. In fact, of course, the AIT embraced ultimately many more policy fields, but the three fields examined here – regional-industrial policy, trade policy, and federal–provincial policy – are those we most need to understand. Later in the chapter we also address the issue of social policy, or the social union, in Canadian federalism, not because this was itself a driving force in the AIT negotiations, but because concern about the social union has been fuelled by the politics governing the debate about free-trade federalism, including the AIT.

The underlying logic of this chapter is that three main developments were cumulatively under way in the 1980s and early 1990s. The first is the relative decline of regional-industrial policy ideas and practises. The second is the aggressive ascendency of trade policy. And the third is the defensive reaction of the federal–provincial policy process in the face of not only the first two developments, but also the very public failures in achieving constitutional renewal through the Meech Lake and the Charlottetown accords. In discussing the framework as a whole, we will refer largely to policy fields, but reference must also be made in each case to 'policy communities,' used in a general sense (Coleman and Skogstad 1990; Pal 1997). In this sense, 'policy communities' is used to discuss the set of players within the various governments and some of the interests involved within each nominal community. However, we are advisedly cautious about arguing that rigidly separate communities can be identified for each field, particularly for the federal–provincial policy field and process. At the same time, however, it is important to see, in the period as a whole, the relative ascendency of the trade field and the trade-policy community and the incursion into federal–provincial policy making of the macro multi–policy field negotiation.

The actual histories of the three fields are complex, and the discussions below endeavour to bring these histories together briefly but with reasonable respect for the subtleties involved. We then turn our attention briefly to the reactive counter-play of the debate about the social union as the new 'economic union' focus of free-trade federalism worked its way through the 1990s.

Regional-Industrial Policy

The first policy field we examine is regional-industrial policy as practised in the previous three decades by both the federal and the provincial governments. The twin areas of regional and industrial policy have policy histories that are linked but not identical. Regional policy set by the federal government has been primarily associated with the use of federal grants to help remove disparities among regions. But the provinces, as chapter 5 will further show, also practised such policies for some of their intraprovincial 'have not' regions. Industrial policy tends to have a somewhat longer history, in the sense that it has been associated with initiatives to promote Canadian manufacturing industries through devices which range from the high-tariff 'national policy' of Sir John A. Macdonald, to policies in the 1960s and 1970s to control foreign investment, to sectoral initiatives for such sectors as auto and textile production (Eden and Molot 1993). Provincial industrial policy involved an array of devices (from grants to procurement, to Crown corporations) to support local industries, which in many provinces were more likely to be natural resource–based (Chandler and Chandler 1979). But as the nature of the economy changed, service sectors also became more and more important for both federal and provincial industrial policies (Statistics Canada 1996).

In this initial mapping of the regional-industrial policy terrain, we have conspicuously omitted trade policy as such. We have done so primarily because there are good reasons for analysing it separately, but, of course, in practice the two types of policies are always linked. Thus, for example, it is important to note that industrial and regional policy grants increased in the 1960s and 1970s precisely because tariffs – the earlier, preferred industrial-policy lever of choice – were coming down under trade policy and GATT-centred auspices (Hart 1994; Doern and Tomlin 1991a).

For the purposes of this brief history, what is crucial is that, as the AIT agenda began to emerge, the 'regional' paradigm and its various versions of addressing and reducing regional disparity increasingly came under attack from several sources of pressure and argument (Savoie 1986; McFetridge 1985; McGee 1992). Indeed, throughout their heyday, regional policies were always in tension with national economic-development policies, if the latter were thought of as policies seeking to maximize overall Canadian GNP through a strong manufacturing sector.

Given that in 1994 the AIT negotiations were being led by Industry Canada, it is useful to review some aspects of the history of this regional–national tension around the various efforts to strike an appropriate mandate for industrial policy. From the 1970s to the early 1990s, several reorganizations and policy changes occurred which variously sought to accommodate these twin pulls of Canada's efforts to devise industrial policies.

From 1969 to 1982, the regional-policy realm was the preserve of the Department of Regional Economic Expansion (DREE), which functioned mainly through grants and federal–provincial regional-development agreements (Savoie 1986; Phidd and Doern 1978). The industrial-competitiveness mandate was the task of the Department of Industry, Trade and Commerce, whose focal point was the knowledge of its industry-sector branches and its trade commissioners (though the latter were transferred to the Department of External Affairs in 1982). Between 1982 and 1987, the twin aspects of policy, regional and industrial, were merged in one department, the Department of Regional Industrial Expansion (DRIE).

With growing dissatisfaction over the warring within a single department of regional–national tensions, and because of the imperatives of a globalizing economy, the Mulroney government again divided the regional from the provincial roles by creating separate regional agencies and by establishing Industry, Science and Technology Canada (ISTC). This department was formed in 1987, and was given a mandate that, to a greater extent than ever before, was to focus upon international technology-based competitiveness. The government also announced that its new flagship department 'for the micro economy' was to phase down its use of grants (regional and otherwise) and was to base its role much more on good analysis and knowledge. It was also to become, internally within the government, a reasoned advocate for industrial competitiveness – in short, a more aggressive horizontal agency across the federal government. ISTC and its predecessor departments had suffered a decline in influence as well, a fact reflected in the frequent changes in ministers, nine in a decade. But for most of the period being reviewed here, the industry departments did have money. Indeed, on an annual basis it was probably the largest amount of discretionary funding available in Ottawa (Doern 1990).

The availability of money, and the capacity to subsidize or protect industry, were, however, already on a steep downhill path. Budget cuts in the department had been significant in the early 1990s, and new FTA, NAFTA, and GATT–WTO trade rules had further blunted the ability to employ subsidies as policy tools. When Industry Canada (the current department) was formed in 1993 out of yet another reorganization, regional policy concerns and money to support them were already on a clear downward trajectory.

For their part, the provincial governments had their own versions of this kind of history. Provincial industrial policies were frequently designed in the 1960s and 1970s as 'province-building' initiatives (Tupper 1986; Dunn 1996; Chandler and Chandler 1979). But the lead player or department varied across the provinces, as determined, in part, by the nature of the dominant industries in each province. Each province had an industrial- or economic-development ministry, but frequently other departments were the de facto provincial government lead players. Thus, in Alberta, energy departments were central, as was the forestry ministry in British Columbia (Doern and Toner 1985; Drushka 1985).

Provincial industrial policies evolved as well through a variety of devices, from subsidies to local procurement preferences, but also through the use of provincial Crown corporations and investment funds (Tupper and Doern 1988). The government enterprises often centred around the provincial hydros or electricity firms but extended as well to a broader range of 'Crowns,' as in the case of Saskatchewan, and to other resource sectors in a province, depending on which resource sector was important there (e.g., oil and gas, coal, mining, forestry, fisheries). Quebec's reliance on state-owned firms and investment funds was cast as an integrated 'Quebec Inc.' approach (Courchene 1992; Courchene and Stewart 1992).

As the time for the AIT negotiations approached, the provinces adopted a view of the underlying economy that was a mixture of real trading trends in the 1990s and aspects of policy thinking that looked towards the regional and provincial industrial-policy traditions and institutions of the past. The latter were under attack, but they had not disappeared from the consciousness of governments and their negotiators as the AIT process began.

Given the domestic policy history sketched above, and the context of the already evident free-trade climate, the federal government's AIT goals and strategies in 1993–4 were necessarily mixed. At one level, federal strategy was to push hard for the removal of as many barriers as possible simply because this made general economic sense. However, at another, more compelling level, the federal agenda was driven by the logic and pressures of the FTA, NAFTA, and the then pending GATT–WTO agreements. The underlying competitiveness of the Canadian economy was seen to lie overwhelmingly with the ability to compete internationally in open markets, and hence the internal market could be no less open. The federal government, however, could not take a totally consistent free trade–oriented position because it, too, had concerns and obligations regarding regional economic development, and hence some of its own barriers were at stake.

Trade Policy

As we have seen, trade policy had always conditioned regional-industrial policy, but it also has its own separate and distinct history. Trade policy had by definition been an internationally oriented activity (Hart 1993; Doern and Tomlin 1991a; 1996), but the basic thrust of its history over the previous two decades has been its increasing focus on issues that heretofore were seen as domestic or internal matters (Hart 1993; Wade 1990; Oakley 1990). In one sense, Canadian trade policy can be interpreted as the pursuit of the long-term goal of general trade liberalization, and from this perspective it has a longer post–Second World War 'freer trade' trajectory (McFetridge 1985; Blais 1985). However, as it travelled this path, trade policy underwent several discernible changes (Doern and Tomlin 1996): (1) an accelerated adoption of free trade primarily through bilateral and regional agreements, but also through the GATT; (2) the extension of liberalized trade rules to goods, services, and aspects of investment 'over the border'; (3) the re-energizing and deepening of trade and export promotion policies; (4) the decline of the tariff and spending as policy instruments, and the need to employ knowledge- and service-delivery instruments; and (5) the growing attention to business framework laws. All of these changes were couched, as we see below, in a larger and often intense debate over both sovereignty and economic liberalism, with the latter ascendant and the former on the defensive or in the process of being significantly redefined.

The pursuit of free trade *per se*, first under the FTA and then under

NAFTA, clearly represents the first major change in policy. This change was all the more significant because it involved a relative shift to a bilateral/regional approach to trade policy from the multilateral GATT-centred policy emphasis of the earlier post–Second World War years (Stone 1984). Even with Canadian participation in, and support for, a new GATT arrangement in 1994, there is little doubt that trade policy shifted to a more regional approach over the period as whole (Hart 1994; Doern and Tomlin 1991a).

The second change in trade policy involved a conception of free trade that extended considerably beyond tariffs and measures applied to goods 'at the border' to include more intrusive rules 'across the border' that would be applied as well to services and trade-related investment. Endorsed under the general concept of promoting national treatment (undertakings to treat incoming goods and investment no differently from domestic ones), such policies inevitably involved changes to, and partial collisions with, many other policies which previously were seen to involve domestic-policy levers in other, non–trade policy fields, from agriculture to intellectual property, and from foreign-investment control to environmental and health and safety standards (Boddez and Trebilcock 1993).

A third change in trade policy involved a renewed emphasis on the trade-promotion function of government, accompanied by a redefinition of traditional trade-promotion activities. In one sense, this was a renewal of an old policy emphasis with roots going back to the formation of Canada's Trade Commissioner Service (TCS) in the earliest days of the old Department of Trade and Commerce (Phidd and Doern 1978; Williams 1983). However, trade promotion was given a new focus, in that the TCS would have to adapt in order to service firms that are either going global or being globalized because of incoming competition.

Trade policy also changed in a fourth way, and here we reconnect with our discussion of industrial policy. The tariff, the earliest instrument of trade-industrial policy and the centrepiece of John A. Macdonald's National Policy, has been virtually eliminated with regard to North American trade. Furthermore, procedures to review the use of subsidies and trade remedies significantly limit the policy room available to governments to favour national firms or industries (Harris 1993; Eden and Molot 1993).

In the 1950s and 1960s, federal trade policy supported a more liberal international trade regime, even as it developed programs for various sectoral and infrastructure-based targets of policy, including the 'managed trade' package known as the Auto Pact. This occurred within the context of high but declining tariffs, moderate subsidization, and relatively deep federal budgetary pockets. In the 1970s and early 1980s, while tariffs went down further and some new non-tariff barriers were erected (e.g., import quotas and voluntary export-restraint agreements), federal industrial policy was cast, as we have seen, much more explicitly in terms of regions and sectors (Savoie 1986). As tariff protection went down, expenditure subsidies and industrial-policy grants went up, at least as long as federal money was available. The provinces, too, seeking to create regionally vital industries in the name of province-building, engaged in the spending version of sectoral/regional industrial policy (Tupper 1986).

Fifth, federal trade policy has witnessed a renewed focus on business framework laws. Such laws, which regulate competition policy, intellectual property, corporate governance, and the like, have always been a part of domestic policy. However, the new focus, especially following NAFTA and the GATT arrangements of the 1990s, is on how to link and harmonize international framework regimes in these areas to traditional trade policy (Doern 1996; Industry Canada 1994).

Recent analyses suggest that these regulatory framework laws are rich in potential for international capitalist 'system frictions.' 'System friction' is the term given by Sylvia Ostry to a new form of international discord, which she argued in 1990 was much broader than protectionism (Ostry 1990, 1993). The term 'underlined that there were several different market models among capitalist economies, the differences stemming from both historical and cultural legacies as well as divergence in a range of domestic policies' (Ostry 1993, 2). These different models influenced the international competitiveness of firms, where competitiveness was the product of an 'interaction between the firm's own capabilities and the broad institutional context of its home country' (p. 2). These frictions had to be reduced through harmonization of those policies that affected a firm's innovative capability. Ostry went on to argue that a key focus would have to be on the issue of 'effective market access,' a concept which she acknowledged to be 'soft and even slippery' and which, at its core, was at the blurred boundaries of competition, trade, investment, intellectual property, and 'high tech industrial policy.' Ostry cast her arguments in the context of political realities among 'the Triad' of trading/political blocs: the European Union, United States–North America, and Japan–Pacific. These system frictions involve regulatory framework laws which are directed, not at governments *per se*, but rather at business firms themselves (Albert 1993; de la Mothe and Paquet 1996).

Often practitioners of such policies see themselves as operating in largely 'domestic' areas of policy that are embedded in different national capitalist traditions. However, these areas are already partially captured in the new GATT, and would certainly be even more fully captured in the next GATT–WTO Round, for which an agenda is already forming. Many, if not most, of these framework areas are now, in departmental terms, a part of Industry Canada. It is worth noting that the Department of Foreign Affairs and International Trade (DFAIT)is also encountering pressures for changes in the international rules about framework business laws – not only directly, but also through similar pressures within various international and regional bodies such as the Organization for Economic Cooperation and Development (OECD), the WTO, and various international sectoral regulators and regimes (Doern 1995a; Doern and Wilks 1996).

The broad nature of these changes also affects how one views the trade-policy community. Until the early to mid 1980s, the trade-policy community was actually quite small and had functioned in a closed circle, centred around the basic rhythm of activity governed by the periodic multi-year GATT rounds (Protheroe 1980; Hart 1993). In the 1960s and 1970s Kennedy and Tokyo GATT rounds, relatively compact trade delegations went off to Geneva or elsewhere to negotiate trade deals. They of course had negotiating mandates from their ministers, but, during this period, negotiations focused primarily on the tariff and related matters, and thus directly concerned only a small number of players. There were links to the business community, but nothing that approached the system adopted and needed in the 1980s and 1990s. The provinces were not a key part of this process either, until the FTA and NAFTA.

This relatively sequestered existence for the trade-policy community changed markedly from the mid-1980s on, when the FTA, NAFTA, and Uruguay GATT–WTO negotiations occurred. First, these negotiations as a whole were virtually continuous from 1985 to 1994. Second, as indicated above, they grew in scope (compared with earlier GATT rounds) to encompass areas of public policy that were previously seen as national, domestic, and, in essence, non–trade-oriented. Hence the trade-policy community was necessarily far larger. Third, these negotiations were accompanied by quite elaborate sectoral consultations with business through the Sectoral Advisory Groups on International Trade (SAGITs) (Doern and Tomlin 1991a; Hart 1994). Fourth, the trade negotiations also included federal–provincial consultation processes that were quite combative in the FTA negotiations, and somewhat smoother in the

NAFTA and GATT negotiations. Fifth, during these negotiations, the federal government's trade negotiation office and its team, became, in a certain sense, a 'mini-government' in that power and influence coalesced around it as it negotiated, within a Cabinet mandate, a set of policies cast in the name of 'trade' policy but in fact involving many areas of domestic policy in the domain of several ministers and departments, and involving directly and indirectly more areas of provincial concern and jurisdiction.

By the end of this ten-year continuous trade-negotiation process, and as the 1994 internal-trade negotiations began, the enlarged trade-policy community was flush with success, confident and aggressive and determined to extend trade concepts and thinking into wider realms. It was a policy community that had some familiarity with federal–provincial relations. As mentioned, the more 'domestic' trade had become, the more provincial jurisdictions were affected. However, at the same time, the trade-policy community was not enmeshed in the traditions, memories, and lexicon of the federal–provincial policy community.

Above all, the trade-policy community was used to an explicit negotiation-centred mode of decision making with several important features. First, there were multiple players engaged in trade-offs across a wide range of policy fields. Indeed, the definition of free trade under GATT meant that agreements had to be broadly based and comprehensive. If not, all that one would have is sectoral trade or managed trade agreements which were hard to negotiate precisely because interest groups that opposed them could focus their energies around the defeat of the initiative. The second feature of the negotiating mode was a reasonably clear sense of a deadline with political muscle behind it. In the case of the FTA and NAFTA, the discipline was undoubtedly supplied by the U.S. 'fast track' process on trade deals which set deadlines for the president to receive a proposal and present it to Congress. There it could be voted on as a deal in total, rather than picked apart by brokerage-based congressional politics. In the case of the GATT–WTO Uruguay Round, the U.S. process again supplied the discipline, but the European Union and Japan also influenced the setting of the deadline date. The final feature of the negotiation mode is that trade-policy makers thought very explicitly about negotiating strategies, regarding what to offer, and when, and what had to be given up. We return to this point in the next section, on federal–provincial policy making, because, among other things, there are issues that arise in negotiation that depend on what the nature of the negotiating game is in terms of trade policy and federal–provincial relations.

Federal–Provincial Policy

It is widely understood that aspects of federalism either directly or indirectly affect nearly all Canadian policy making (McRoberts 1993; Painter 1991). The recent experience of the negotiations for the Agreement on Internal Trade is clearly no exception to this rule. Not only does the agreement itself represent a new framework for an enhanced Canadian economic union within existing federal structures, but the process whereby negotiations took place were yet another example of federalism at work. In fact, as then Quebec premier Daniel Johnson stated, the AIT represented a 'perfect illustration of how federalism should work' (quoted in Schwartz 1995, 214).

Thus, of the three fields examined in this chapter, federal–provincial policy is in many respects the largest and most amorphous. After all, there are probably well over forty policy areas in which the federal and provincial governments engage in some form of joint or coordinated policy process. What, then, is 'normal' federal–provincial policy making, or federalism at work? This question is important in that one of the overall arguments in this book is that federal–provincial policy making is not normally characterized by macro multi–policy field negotiations and that the AIT was different in requiring the latter approach.

But how can one tell what federal–provincial policy making is like? One of the problems here is that, in the literature on federalism, the actual policy process is usually a secondary consideration, coming well behind the larger political and constitutional concerns of the authors, and also well behind judgments of the basic shifting balance of power between the two levels of government. In terms of the discussion of federalism's normal decision making, there are three basic kinds of analysis: (a) general observations about the nature of decision making; (b) discussions of constitutional reform processes; and (c) policy-field case studies.

Among the general conceptions of federal–provincial policy making, two come to mind in this context. The first centres on executive federalism, and the second focuses on multilateral versus bilateral federal–provincial relations. Even the newest student of Canadian politics will have been introduced to the central concepts of 'executive federalism' and its accompanying notions of decision making through 'elite accommodation.' In Canada, executive federalism has been shown to emerge out of our relatively decentralized system (Smiley 1980; Cairns 1977). The result is an elaborate policy-making system characterized by secretive administrative, ministerial, and first-ministerial meetings, and bargains in those areas that have cross-jurisdictional impact. Executive federalism has also been characterized as a form of diplomatic bargaining analogous to that which takes place between sovereign states at the international level (Simeon 1972; Schultz 1980).

The concept of bilateral versus multilateral federalism focuses on asymmetrical features (McRoberts 1985). In short, federalism can yield policy fields where, at any given time, the decision process could involve, in different combinations, the federal government dealing with one province, or groups of provinces, or all of them. Such negotiations may still be done in the secretive executive-federalism mode, but this observation about decision making adds an important subtlety.

The second type of observation about federalism and decision making focuses on processes for constitutional policy making that may be linked to the general modes of thinking noted above. Perhaps the archetypal example of executive federalism at work in the previous ten years is that involving the Meech Lake Accord. Negotiated entirely behind closed doors by the eleven First Ministers of the time, the Meech Accord represented constitution-building by secrecy. The story of Meech has been told elsewhere and need not be recounted here (Cohen 1990; Campbell and Pal 1991). What is important is the lesson for executive federalism that has been drawn from Meech. Notwithstanding the 'success' in actually negotiating the accord, most commentators have stressed the lack of public input and participation as the ultimate cause of its downfall (Watts 1989b; Brock 1991). As Richard Simeon points out, 'the process was seen as elitist and unaccountable; the participants were seen to be unrepresentative; the process was illegitimate; and the Constitution had come to be seen as the property not of governments, or even of legislatures, but of "the people"' (1990, 30).

The view that emerged as a result of the Meech failure was one that sought to address the lack of citizen participation in federal–provincial policy making of such magnitude as constitutional negotiations. The need for change was a given. Some argued that constitutional amendment would require greater public input and legitimacy, but that the elite bargaining process typically ascribed to executive federalism was still necessary, although perhaps in a modified form, with the involvement of third-party arbitrators (Stein 1989). Others sought the coordination of ideas from public groups, governments, and the variety of committees that had been struck to address constitutional issues in concert with a more visible and open process of dialogue (Brock 1991). Common to all, however, was the notion that a process other than that of the Meech Lake experience was necessary for constitutional federalism to work.

During the second constitutional debate of the previous ten years, the Charlottetown Accord and the failure of the national referendum on its acceptance, attempts were made to reshape the processes of federalism. A considerable effort was mounted to include as many previously excluded groups as possible. The series of 'town hall' meetings, the various joint committees on constitutional renewal, and the ratification process itself were all evidence of a move away from the traditional strictures of executive federalism. And although the Charlottetown operation has been classified as an 'amoebic' process that 'groped' towards an agreement, with little direct foresight (Young and Brown 1992), it must be concluded that it was entirely a more open and multilateral experience when compared with that of Meech. The final outcome, of course, was not all that different, and is perhaps evidence that, although a more open exercise, Charlottetown nonetheless typified a process of 'elite accommodation.' The lesson learned was that mechanisms for negotiating outside the executive level, but still very much within federalism, could be 'technically' successful, even if not successful in entrenchment. It can be reasonably argued that in the post-Meech era then, including during the Charlottetown process, the status quo of Canadian federalism and its effect on policy-making mechanisms had undergone a modification, although not a transformation. The Charlottetown constitutional policy-making processes did involve some experimentation with separate negotiating tables on different topics (though not policy fields, as was the case in the AIT process), and of course it was cast as a negotiation.

The third source on which to base analysis of federal–provincial policy processes is policy case studies. Virtually every book devoted to a policy field in Canada makes some reference to federalism, but such studies typically do not have federal–provincial decision processes as their focal point. They more often focus on the political executive and key departments, and on the interest-group structure. This literature presents a varied view of what one can infer about federal–provincial processes. For example, energy policy was cast as having some bargaining/negotiation elements in 1980 (especially bilateral relations between the federal government and Alberta) because it was linked initially to a secretive Budget Speech deadline (Doern and Toner 1985). But energy policy also included many other forms of 'normal' decision making of the executive-federalism and multilateral kind. Another example is agricultural policy, which involves a field of concurrent jurisdiction (Skogstad 1987).

Skogstad's several analyses of agriculture policy and politics again show a variety of decision-making modes and processes.

While each of these kinds of evidence of, and characterizations of, the federal–provincial process suggests the need for caution, none indicates that multi–policy field negotiations as such are normal in the federal–provincial policy process.

One other obvious area to explore is previous trade agreements and the extent of federal–provincial interaction involved in them. The traditional forms of executive federalism and federal–provincial relations had been pivotal during the negotiations of the Canada–United States. FTA and the subsequent NAFTA, and the Uruguay Round of the GATT. Given the reality that negotiating an international-trade agreement of the magnitude of the FTA required the federal government to bargain in some related areas of provincial jurisdiction, coupled with the increasingly important nature of the internationalization of domestic policies at both the federal and the provincial levels, it should not be surprising that federalism had an impact on foreign-trade policy. The essence of this effect was to establish trade policy to 'reflect domestic considerations of a federal constitution and political culture, and a strongly regionalised economy with a long tradition of competing trade interests' (Brown 1989, 212). Such a policy worked at two levels.

First, it established expertise in trade issues among officials, both elected and administrative, in the provinces. Although, as suggested earlier, this community was relatively small, it gained considerable experience, particularly in areas of provincial jurisdiction.

Second, it opened discussion between federal and provincial officials about trade issues. In large part this relationship was restricted to dialogue, or to an advocacy role for the provinces, since executive federalism with respect to trade policy was not a well-established decision-making process (although we outline later the increasing pressure put on the federal government by the provinces for their inclusion). In fact, even given the provincial role, the federal government still retained the jurisdiction to act unilaterally in matters of foreign-trade policy (Brown 1989). As a result, some have indicated that the federal government was able to negotiate trade provisions – for example, in NAFTA – that appear to favour a federal, rather than provincial, power grab by way of policy-instrument limitations (Robinson 1993). Such a conclusion would appear to support a traditional view of non-cooperative or confrontational federalism. Others, however, have argued quite the opposite, suggesting that the increasing provincial role in trade policy has actually resulted in instances where federal–provincial cooperation is the norm (Skogstad 1996). What is clear is that the provinces have gained an increased, and increasing, role in national trade policy, a fact that is a result of, and has implications for, Canadian federalism (Robinson 1995).

Given the new role for the provinces in trade policy, it was perhaps not surprising that, shortly after the experience with international free trade, calls were made once again for the liberalization of internal trade within Canada (Palda 1994; Norrie, Simeon, and Krasnick 1986). Such calls could be seen as an effort to resolve the paradox of Canadian trade policy – free trade abroad, restricted trade at home (Schwartz 1995). What is somewhat surprising, as chapter 3 shows in more detail, is that it took a strictly federal initiative to get the internal-trade ball rolling. In part, this was due to the relative obscurity of the issue as a policy concern at the provincial level of government, but perhaps equally important was a general reluctance to enter into another round of 'executive federalism,' given the Meech and Charlottetown experiences. In essence, then, a rebirth of Canadian federalism was required.

If the Meech Lake Accord and the FTA are perceived as illustrative case studies in Canadian federalism, and the subsequent Charlottetown, NAFTA, and GATT procedures are seen as further examples of or slight modifications to the status quo, then, in one way, the AIT period can be viewed as a major change. The difference is not at the 'executive' level, for indeed the AIT was very much an executive exercise, but rather at the process or negotiating level. While traditional visions of executive federalism have focused on the role of bargaining and negotiation as the mechanism for the resolution of intergovernmental matters in a general way (Watts 1989b), they have done so without reference to the burgeoning literature on negotiations (Stein 1989).

Even when bargaining has been explicitly analysed in collective decision or policy making in Canadian federalism, it has subscribed to the literature on game theory that offers us a model of cooperative executive federalism based on the 'solution' of the classic Prisoner's Dilemma (PD) game (Brander 1985). However, as Albert Breton (1985) has correctly pointed out, the PD game cannot be used as a model for federalism for two reasons. In the first place, governments are not held incommunicado, as is required by the PD game. Second, and more important, the PD analysis of federalism assumes that governments are perfect representatives of their citizens' interests. When one relaxes this assumption, as it is certainly reasonable (if not necessary) to do, intergovernmental cooperation can lead to inefficient outcomes (Breton 1985).

Another of the shortcomings of the game-theoretic approach offered by Brander (1985) in the study of Canadian federalism can actually be linked to the 'case' material available for study. Prior to the negotiation of the AIT, there had been no case in Canadian intergovernmental relations where an issue that captured multi-party bargaining about multi-policy field issues at the executive level had also included a formal negotiating structure involving both firm time constraints and the actions of a third-party arbitrator (in the person of Arthur Mauro) and a consensus-building administrative party in the form of the Internal Trade Secretariat (see chapter 3). As Stein (1989) intimated, such a bargaining process would have considerable effect on the method of communication, and eventually on the policy output. It is the introduction of these additional variables that represents the most significant departure from previous forms of executive federalism, and leads us to the conclusion that the AIT process offers a new 'model' of federalism melded to a mode of trade-style negotiations across a multi–policy field terrain.

The AIT process represented a degree of formality in negotiations that had previously been absent in federal–provincial relations. This formality can be seen to have emerged out of the failures of prior decision-making efforts, but, perhaps more important, it was quite simply 'designed.' As we show further in chapter 3, there was widespread belief among all AIT negotiators that the process itself, including the neutral chair, the role of the ITS, and the adherence to a strict deadline, was a significant contributor to the eventual success in reaching agreement.

The formal analysis of intergovernmental relations has mainly focused on the sort of game-theoretic modelling that Brander (1985) has offered. In particular, numerous studies have shown how international military diplomacy can be modelled using two-party, single-issue, zero-sum games such as the Prisoner's Dilemma, and games of deterrence and tit-for-tat (e.g., Rapoport and Chammah 1965; Brams 1985; Axelrod 1984). More recently, however, studies have begun to indicate that rarely (if ever) is it appropriate to treat intergovernmental relations in this manner, because of the non–zero-sum characteristics of many relationships in the public sphere. The non–zero-sum analysis of intergovernmental relations allows for the mixed motivations of the players (i.e., situations where the players have both competitive and cooperative interests), and it can lead to cooperative games where the players can coordinate their strategies through binding agreements (Morrow 1994, 76). The addition of multi-issue space and multi-party bargaining complicates matters further (Raiffa

1982). It is clear that the AIT process closely matched the non–zero-sum, cooperative, multi-issue, multilateral case.

The AIT case also adds two other variables to the mix: the neutral chair (and the ITS, which is probably reasonably viewed as a direct extension of the chair), and the finite game structure. These two new institutions introduced to policy making in Canadian federal–provincial relations both had positive effects (as measured by the successful negotiation of the AIT). The role of the mediator was twofold. First, the mediator acted to bring the parties together as they attempted to reconcile, in this case, thirteen different interests in fifteen policy fields. Second, by acting as the 'go-between,' the neutral chair not only kept the process running, but was able to mediate/induce a fair compromise among the parties with respect to their interests (Young 1991; Brams, Kilgour, and Merrill 1991). The chair helped structure an agreement.

Imposing a finite time-line on the AIT process also had an effect on the success of the negotiations. With an end-game always in mind, and given the non–zero-sum nature of the cooperative game, parties had an incentive eventually to reveal final-offer positions that were likely to result in compromise. And even though this compromise was not secured, as is normal in trade negotiations, until the 'eleventh hour,' the finite nature of the game resulted in agreement.

The AIT process is thus seen as a new step in the development of intergovernmental relations in Canadian federalism. By approaching the negotiations with new institutions and 'rules of the game,' the governments were able to reach compromise on a national scale through trade-offs across a large number of policy fields.

The Social Union: The Missing Dimension?

While the framework of three changing and converging policy fields is the focal point for our analysis of free-trade federalism and of the AIT, it is important to draw attention in this chapter to the emergence of concerns about the Canadian social union, indeed to the deployment of the term 'social union' itself. The AIT was not premised on a direct concern for social policy *per se.* Implicitly, though, the constraints placed on signatories to the agreement in the areas of procurement, labour mobility, consumer-related measures and standards, and environmental protection have potential social-policy implications, especially if one takes a broad view of what social policy actually is. Indeed, some of the provinces, as chapter 4 shows, were quite explicit about such concerns.

Social policy and the social union are secondary subjects in this book, but it is important to introduce here some of the links that are a part of the total fabric of federalism when it is confronted by free-trade impera- tives. The social-union concept seemed to emerge after the AIT was nego- tiated, but there were threads of concern in the earlier Charlottetown Accord and NAFTA processes where a parallel debate about a social char- ter for Canada and the NAFTA 'side agreements' on the environment and labour emerged. In addition, the June 1997 Cabinet appointments following the re-election of the Chrétien government to its second term saw the creation of Cabinet committees for the economic union and the social union after a major review of what the medium-term policies of the federal government ought to be in the next few years. Such a move acknowledges the obvious relationship between the social and the eco- nomic in Cabinet decision making, and in real life, and appears to match the recent vogue for discussing the implications of economic policy on social policy, in an interdependent way. It also reflected a quite deliberate use of terminology related to a 'social union,' much more prevalent in the European Union, and thus showed the broader influence of different global forms of free-trade federalism.

The idea of a social union in its 'pure' form in Canadian federalism is really a debate about the existence (or not) of significant positive social rights in the constitution – in brief, the idea of a Canadian social charter. The most recent experience with this debate occurred during both the Meech Lake and the Charlottetown rounds of constitutional discussion. At its most essential level, the idea of a social charter arose out of the ten- sions inherent in Canadian society regarding the dual political occur- rences of the demise of the social welfare state, and the instability of our constitutional efforts to renew the federation (Bakan and Schneiderman 1992, 2). Those in favour of the idea of a social charter see the opportu- nity for a national social union that lessens the tensions between eco- nomic classes, and grants vulnerable social groups an equal place in society as a right of citizenship (Banting 1988).

Those opposed to the social charter, or at least to those proposals for a social charter that were contained in the debates about the Meech Lake and Charlottetown accords, suggest that the very idea of a constitution- ally guaranteed social union is flawed because of its necessarily ambigu- ous approach and the inability to grant positive rights in a substantive manner (Bakan 1992, 86). This debate continues, and is perhaps tied more directly to the tensions inherent in the Canadian federation between the politics of the federal spending power and the politics of social reform (Banting 1988, 581).

Social policy has also necessarily been linked to the more traditional debates about fiscal federalism in Canada. With the provinces holding key jurisdictional power over social policy, the federal government has been forced to make its attempts at forging a social and economic union through the use of the federal spending power in relation to its obligation for 'peace, order and good government' in Section 91 of the constitution (Savoie 1990, 278). Equalization, the Canada Assistance Plan, Established Program Financing, and the new Canada Health and Social Transfer are all examples of the use of the federal spending power for social policy. However, directly related to the more strictly economic concerns with federal deficits, recent experience suggests that the federal government is much less inclined to use the federal spending power in this way.

Recent commentary has suggested that there is a widening gap between efficiency concerns and equity concerns in the Canadian social and economic union. The broad devolution of power to the provinces from the federal government, coupled with economic difficulties at both jurisdictional levels, appears to be leading towards a more serious imbalance in what some earlier referred to as the federal–provincial social contract (Shoyama 1988). And whereas the decentralization of public-service provision is not at odds with theories of federalism, it appears to present a dilemma for the federal government in that it can affect the national social union only through the use of its spending power – a power that has been muted (Boadway 1995, 203). The effect of this devolution seems to be ever more important, especially as one considers that strong social policy appears to be linked directly to strong economic performance (Courchene 1992, 11). As Shoyama (1988, 160) concludes, 'the loss of competitive power at the broad federal level to countervail against narrower, provincially-based interests, increases the potential for significant welfare loss (in economists' terms) for Canadians as a whole.' While the philosophical base of a social and economic union is strong, the current practical policy options may not be equal to the task.

The Agreement on Internal Trade appears to fit into the debate about a Canadian social and economic union in two ways. In the first place, the AIT, as a framework document for economic union in terms of interprovincial trade, can be viewed as an initial step towards further positive economic integration between jurisdictions in Canadian federalism. We point out that this is a first step, because truly positive economic integration would involve a much more proactive government role for defining economic space and activity than is contained in the AIT (Purvis and Raynauld 1992). However, the agreement does move along a path that enhances the opportunity for economic coordination by limiting barriers to trade. If the AIT works at reducing barriers to innovation in economic performance, particularly with respect to human capital, then the framework aspects of the agreement appear to offer the opportunity for greater social and economic union.

Secondly, the AIT offers a more direct potential for having an impact on the social and economic union through the provisions of the agreement itself. In particular, with respect to areas such as procurement, labour mobility, consumer standards, and the environment, the AIT may well restrict the sort of narrow, provincially defined interests outlined by Shoyama (1988) above, especially through the mutual non-discrimination doctrine (see chapter 4). If the agreement limits the available range of provincial policy instruments in the area of regional economic development, as we believe it does, then it seems safe to conclude that, if these policies were even in part designed to have social effects, then narrowly defined provincial interests may be muted. If Boadway (1995, 203) is correct in asserting that a national social union is out of reach without a strong federal spending power, then the AIT offers some hope in response to the recent trend towards political, geographical, and social decentralization.

This brief discussion of the social union does not do justice to the complex issues of social policy in a federal state. Some elements of a social-union debate are picked up in our account of some of the sectoral negotiating tables, and we return to the social union in our conclusions to the book as a whole.

Conclusions

This chapter has provided a historical and contextual framework both for understanding the presence of free-trade federalism in Canada in the 1990s and for analysing the negotiations that produced the AIT. The broad trajectories of regional-industrial policy, trade policy, and federal–provincial policy have been traced, and an initial sense of the related policy communities has been presented. While each field is complex, the broad pattern of change in the confluence of these fields is quite clear. Trade policy was aggressively in the ascendancy, and crossing borders into the realm of domestic governance, including areas of provincial jurisdiction. Regional-industrial policy was on the defensive and in decline as the global and national micro economy changed, as government budgets shrunk, and as trade rules themselves made old-style regional-industrial policy less and less possible. Federal–provincial policy in its broadest sense was also on the defensive in that the Charlottetown and Meech failures were fresh in mind. Federal–provincial policy formation had experienced a variety of modes of decision making but nothing that approached the style that the AIT was about to involve. A multi–policy field, negotiation-centred form of policy making would be different.

We have also introduced the social-union debate that has become more vigorous since the AIT in order to reinforce the point that the social union and social policy as such were not a key impetus for the AIT. At the same time, the social union is undoubtedly the other side of the coin of free-trade federalism, and hence is an issue to which we return in later parts of this book. In the meantime, we present more of the shorter-term history in chapter 3, in order to explain more precisely how the AIT got on the agenda in the mid-1980s and how the AIT policy process was designed as a negotiation.

3

Getting on the Agenda: Key Stages in the Internal Trade Policy and Negotiation Process

On 18 July 1994, Prime Minister Jean Chrétien announced the signing of the Agreement on Internal Trade (AIT). The prime minister stressed that, 'for the first time, under this new agreement, we will have: clear rules and an impartial dispute settlement mechanism to resolve trade differences between the provinces.' He further pointed out that there was now an 'open procurement process – for all Canadian companies – for the $50 billion spent annually by governments across Canada; and a code of conduct to prevent provinces from luring away investment from each other' (Chrétien 1994, 1).

The simplicity of this statement of key achievements stands in contrast to the difficult journey involved both in getting internal trade on the political agenda and in keeping it there. Prior to dealing with the May and June 1994 final phases of actual negotiations, our focus in chapters 4–8, we need to understand the earlier agenda-setting phases. In effect, these phases can be separated into two periods: the unsuccessful constitutional phase, and the eventually successful non-constitutional phase. While our focus is primarily on the latter phase which spans a ten-year period beginning in the mid-1980s, we begin with a brief comment on the link between earlier constitutional proposals and the AIT.

The chapter, then, looks at an initial but weak push in the 1985–7 period, and then a further period of political momentum in the 1987–93 period. Next it profiles the key negotiating stages in 1993–4, beginning prior to the 1993 election which saw the victory of the Liberals, and extending to the early months of 1994, when a mandate for negotiations was secured and a draft text was made available. Finally, we look at the institutions and arenas of negotiation that were in place by the time of the final phase in May and June 1994 and that paved the way for Prime Minister Chrétien's announcement of the deal.

The Road to the Negotiations

The AIT and the Constitutional Link

Although the AIT is explicitly a non-constitutional agreement, when viewed as an attempt to strengthen the Canadian economic union it has clear political roots that are readily traceable to the constitutional arena. In fact, the idea of a new approach to a common market in Canada dates back to constitutional proposals put forward in the late 1960s, and garnered significant attention during the long period leading up to the patriation of the constitution under the Constitution Act 1982 (Bayefsky 1989, 616–19; Schwanen 1995, 14). This was particularly the case with respect to mobility rights; the movement of goods, services, and capital; and the federal power over trade and commerce. But while some minor changes to the nature of the economic union were guaranteed in 1982, the central constitutional provisions are still maintained by the Constitution Act 1867, sections 91 and 121.

The political debate over the nature of the Canadian domestic market really centres on questions of what *form* the market should take – namely, a customs union, a monetary and economic union. At the heart of this debate is an argument about the degree to which an economic union represents a form of free-trade zone that can be guaranteed by negative integration between jurisdictions, or whether true union also requires positive political integration, perhaps to the extent that joint authority between jurisdictions to formulate and implement economic policy is guaranteed (Lenihan 1995). As the opportunity for some form of greater economic union has been discussed in Canada, it is not surprising that the debate has coincided with broader constitutional questions, and in fact prior to the AIT process described below, it was couched directly in such broader terms.

This link was perhaps most visible during the Canada Round and during the entire period leading to the Charlottetown Accord in 1992. Indeed, significant amendments to sections 91 and 121 were seen as a necessary requirement to a successful round of constitutional negotiations – not only for political reasons, but also as a means of securing future prosperity for Canadians. The successful linkage of economic, social, and constitutional life was viewed as crucial for strengthening the Canadian union (Brown, Lazar, and Schwanen 1992).

As it turned out, however, a direct link between an agreement on the economic union and an agreement on the constitution was not necessary – in large part because the intellectual and political impetus for the reduction of intergovernmental trade barriers in Canada transcended the constitutional arena. And whereas one might reasonably argue that the current AIT could be strengthened by constitutional amendment allowing for a more positive approach to economic integration, the success of the AIT process was, in a very real sense, the result of the decidedly non-constitutional nature of the road to the negotiations.

1985 to 1987: The Push for Internal Trade

As early as 1940, problems relating to internal trade between the federal, provincial, and territorial governments of Canada had been identified (Canada 1940) with a view to reaping efficiency gains in the Canadian internal market. Academic analysis had also certainly suggested that reducing barriers had value (Safarian 1980). However, the push for *policies* to deal with the deleterious effects of internal-trade barriers emerged in a more concerted way from three main sources in the mid-1980s: the economic and policy arguments presented by the Macdonald Commission; the 1985 *Intergovernmental Position Paper on the Principles and Framework for Regional Economic Development;* and the emerging belief in the benefits of reducing barriers to internal trade in the business community and at the political level.

The 1985 *Report of the Royal Commission on the Economic Union and Development Prospects for Canada* (the Macdonald Commission) presented a precise set of arguments about the harmful economic effects of barriers to internal trade (Canada 1985b). While the report offered no exact measure of the economic cost of barriers, the commission argued that the existence of internal-trade impediments was significant and that a conscientious effort should be made to reduce them.

The Macdonald Commission is of interest in two other ways regarding the internal-trade / free-trade links. First, it is useful to remember that there is an explicit connection with Prime Minister Jean Chrétien in the formation of the Macdonald Commission. In the late 1970s, when aggressive provincial governments were challenging federal power, then prime minister Pierre Trudeau assigned Jean Chrétien to examine ways in which there could be a strengthening of the 'Canadian economic union.' This initiative was designed explicitly as a strategy to challenge provincial power and assert federal authority. When the Macdonald Commission was later appointed, half of its title (the Royal Commission on the Economic Union and Development Prospects for Canada) implied the strengthening of the economic union.

The second Macdonald Commission link is related to how internal trade, which was the commission's primary early concern, became of secondary concern, well behind the need for free trade with the United States. When the commission started its work, it asked economists to research internal-trade barriers. The researchers reported that there were barriers, but that they were not significant, especially compared with those inefficiencies in the Canadian economy caused by the absence of free trade with the United States. Thus, as a result of several related arguments and pressures, the 'internal trade' royal commission became the 'free trade' royal commission (Doern and Tomlin 1991a).

The Macdonald Commission's discussion of internal trade became one of several of its secondary recommendations. Perhaps more important than its identification of the economic impacts of internal-trade barriers was the indication that a *political* rationale for barrier reduction also existed. As the commission stated: 'Above the economic rationale, the political rationale for the national right to free movement has a powerful attraction for most Canadians. For a producer to find it easier to sell in another country than in another province offends our sense of Canadianism' (Canada 1985b, 135). By linking the economic and political rationales for barrier reduction, the Macdonald Commission was explicitly arguing for a policy on internal economic conduct.

The Macdonald Commission also proposed a specific process through which such a 'Code of Economic Conduct' might be developed. In particular, the commission suggested that the policy process be based on negotiations between governments:

The principal vehicle both for initiating the development of a Code of Economic Conduct and for implementing it should be a federal–provincial Council of Ministers for Economic Development, established under the umbrella of the First Ministers' Conference. This ministerial council would be assisted by a Federal–Provincial Commission on the Canadian Economic Union consisting of a group of experts appointed by the Council. (Canada 1985b, 138)

As we see below, the process proposed by the Macdonald Commission bears some resemblance to the process that was finally agreed upon by First Ministers in 1993.

Mirroring the recommendations of the Macdonald Commission, a 1985 intergovernmental paper, *On the Principles and Framework for Regional Economic Development*, was released that focused on the principle of recognizing that Canadian economic efficiency and social equity are the responsibility of all political jurisdictions. In particular, the eighth principle of the paper suggested that 'governments should explore opportunities for increasing interregional trade and eliminating barriers between provinces' (Canada 1985a, 13).

The intergovernmental position paper represented the first time that all Canadian governments had given serious attention to internal trade as a significant policy issue. The product of work by the Committee of Regional Economic Development Ministers (CREDM), the position paper indicated that barriers to intergovernmental trade should be considered important in the context of both regional and national economic policy – a first in federal–provincial economic-development initiatives. In addition, the CREDM established a task force of officials, co-chaired by Saskatchewan and the federal government, to develop policy options for the implementation of the eighth principle, an important first step towards bureaucratically institutionalizing internal-trade policy in federal–provincial collaborations. However, it was not until political awareness about barriers to trade were raised that significant efforts for their reduction were initiated.

One of the crucial reasons for the sluggishness of the internal-trade issue was obviously that not only was it number eight in the regional-policy list, but it was even lower on the larger priority list of governments. In the case of the federal government, the agenda in the 1986–8 period was undoubtedly dominated by the Canada–United States free-trade issue (Doern and Tomlin 1991a). But in the larger context of a federalism agenda, internal trade was also on the lower rungs of the policy ladder. Federalism was itself preoccupied eventually with the Meech Lake process (Abele 1991; Courchene 1991), but also with the already serious concerns about federal budgetary cutbacks, especially those related to social programs in the Mulroney Conservative era (Courchene 1987; Banting 1988).

However, as the awareness of barriers to internal trade grew between 1985 and 1987, it was only a matter of time before the issue garnered attention in the political community as well. Two types of pressure began to boost the issue up the policy-agenda ladder. First, pressure from national business lobbies increased in concert with the larger free-trade agenda. One form of this pressure came through studies of the economic costs of internal-trade barriers to the Canadian economy as a whole. These studies looked at both static and dynamic costs, and produced widely varying estimates, from hundreds of million to several billion dollars (Schwanen 1995, 5; Copeland 1993; Palda 1994). The studies and accompanying business pressure produced reactions of both support and scepticism from the provinces, which continued into the negotiation process.

A second form of learning-curve pressure came from internal bureaucratic studies and processes. In the early stages, for example, sector-specific issues were raised. For instance, in 1986 Statistics Canada was commissioned to present a report on government procurement and investment as an instrument of regional economic policy (Department of Regional Economic Expansion, 21 February 1986). As time passed, however, a more comprehensive political understanding of interprovincial barriers as a whole emerged. At the 27th Annual Premiers' Conference, held in Edmonton on August 10–12, 1986, the premiers endorsed a set of four initiatives designed to steer efforts for barrier reduction:

– a broad best-efforts moratorium on new barriers subject to compelling considerations of provincial economic development
– a permanent mechanism to reduce barriers
– a process to validate an inventory of barriers
– a set of guiding principles for reducing barriers (Premiers' Conference 1986).

These four principles represented a strong statement from the premiers about internal trade, and were instrumental in initiating the development of an eighteen-month joint federal–provincial work plan to consider barriers in four economic sectors (government procurement, marketing practices for alcoholic beverages, transportation regulations, and employment practices), and to propose to First Ministers that a committee of portfolio ministers be mandated to deal specifically with issues of internal trade (Department of Regional Economic Expansion, 29 October 1986). More than anything else, it was this political impetus that truly started the internal-trade ball rolling.

1987 to 1993: Developing Institutions and a Framework for Negotiations

Between 1987 and 1993, institutions and a general framework for internal-trade negotiations emerged out of a series of collaborations between the federal and provincial governments and their officials. Based on the premise that barriers to internal trade were economically inefficient and ran counter to political beliefs about the freedom of economic activity within Canada, the negotiation framework institutionalized a federal–provincial policy process for trade-barrier reduction, established a set of principles and applications for internal trade, and made explicit the rules for the negotiation of an agreement.

Institutional Development

The institutionalization of internal trade began in earnest in November 1987, when First Ministers established the Committee of Ministers on Internal Trade (CMIT) with responsibilities for

– continuing identification of existing barriers to efficient and balanced internal trade in Canada;
– receiving representations from individuals, businesses, industry associations and governments concerning new and existing government policies, programs, regulations and practices which they believe impede trade in Canada;
– examining barriers identified through research and representation and reducing and removing such barriers through consultation and appropriate negotiation and mediation processes; and
– reporting to First Ministers on internal trade conditions in Canada and on their efforts to reduce or remove barriers to interprovincial trade. (Industry, Science and Technology Canada 1987)

The committee was also charged with an initial list of sector-specific areas for immediate attention: government procurement, liquor-board marketing practices, and transportation regulations. For the first time, a dedicated intergovernmental ministerial committee, armed with a clear mandate and resources for its accomplishment, was working in the internal-trade policy field. Not only was this development significant in terms of keeping the policy issue in the public eye and on the intergovernmental agenda, it also established a lasting forum for governments, officials, and Canadians to monitor, and participate in, the internal-trade policy debate. Importantly, internal trade had been institutionalized.

Between 1987 and 1993, the CMIT directed its primary efforts towards conceptualizing a comprehensive framework for internal-trade negotiations. This framework was not finalized until late 1992, when it was announced that full-fledged negotiations were to begin (Committee of Ministers on Internal Trade 1992). However, in the intervening years, the CMIT played an integral role in directing the sector-specific negotiations outlined above. This activity was important for two main reasons. First, the implementation of the Intergovernmental Agreements on Beer Marketing and Government Procurement (Internal Trade Secretariat 1994) and the Memorandum of Understanding on a set of national standards for transportation vehicles indicated a first step forward. Although these agreements were limited in their scope and effectiveness, a signal was sent by the CMIT that intergovernmental negotiations were possible and that the institution that had been developed for this process was capable of facilitating agreements. Second, with some sector-specific successes in hand, the CMIT was able to strengthen its efforts towards setting a more broadly focused agenda.

On 4 December 1992, the CMIT announced an agreement to accelerate the comprehensive internal-trade negotiations. After having been directed by First Ministers to complete an internal-trade agreement by 31 March 1995, the CMIT held a series of meetings to establish the principles and applications that were to guide the comprehensive negotiations (see below). At the 4 December 1992 CMIT meeting, it was also agreed that each government would discuss the principles and applications with respect to their jurisdiction and then report their findings back to the CMIT. To aid this process, a task force was formed comprising officials from each jurisdiction, supported by Industry, Science and Technology Canada (now Industry Canada).

The formation of an interim bureaucratic institution for internal trade established, for the first time, an official administrative structure to aid the negotiations. At a meeting of the task force on 17 December 1992, discussion related to the steps officials were, or would be, taking to ascertain their respective government's response to the CMIT proposal, what the process of negotiations would entail in organizational and logistical terms, and the areas or sectors to be addressed (Interim Secretariat 1992).

On 18 March 1993, the CMIT announced that comprehensive internal-trade negotiations would begin by 1 July 1993, with an objective of reaching an agreement by 30 June 1994 (Committee of Ministers on Internal Trade 1993). At the same time, a proposal was put forth regarding the institutions that would structure the negotiations. And while these institutions were refined over the next few months, a general framework had been set (see figure 1).

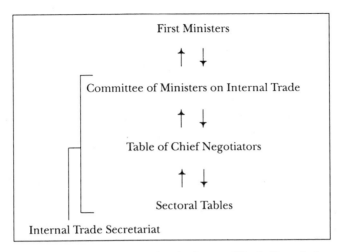

Figure 1: General Structure for the Internal-Trade Negotiations

The ultimate authority for developing the Agreement on Internal Trade lay with the customary executive-federalism institution of First Ministers. The granting of this authority was in large part a function of the intergovernmental nature of the policy, but can also be viewed as a natural extension of the traditional federal–provincial policy-making process. However, unlike many previous intergovernmental policy efforts, the internal-trade process was also supported by a new set of institutions designed specifically to deal with policy making through negotiation between jurisdictions.

In order to make such a cross-jurisdictional policy process work as effectively as possible, a neutral chair for the negotiations (Winnipeg lawyer Arthur Mauro) was appointed in August 1993. As chapter 4 shows in more detail, his role was to ensure that jurisdictional issues were dealt with in a cooperative manner. Indeed, one of the driving forces behind the agreement was the realization in many quarters that greater inter-jurisdictional cooperation was necessary to improve the efficiency of the Canadian economy overall.

The design of the table of chief negotiators, with representatives from all of the governments in Canada, expressly reflected this underlying philosophy and represented an innovative, though not totally unprecedented, approach to federal–provincial policy making. The Charlottetown negotiations had involved a fairly elaborate array of tables, albeit not organized on the basis of policy fields. It also had a secretariat. In the

AIT negotiations, each participant relied on resources from its particular jurisdiction to inform specific negotiating stances. At the central table, though, the negotiating process was supported by an Internal Trade Secretariat, which, although staffed and paid for by the federal government, reported to the neutral chair and was separate and distinct from the federal chief negotiator, Andrei Sulzenko. The role of the secretariat was to provide research, and analytical and administrative support, for the negotiations. As a bureaucratic agency, the secretariat was intended to function with political impartiality and provide the negotiations with a stable 'inner voice.'

The institutional framework for the internal-trade negotiations proved to be quite effective. The substance of the negotiations was completed in the main through work done by groups of negotiators at the sectoral tables. Usually one jurisdiction accepted the role of chair for this work, supported either by its own resources or by the central secretariat. In this way, responsibility was distributed among all parties, with provinces functioning as the lead on a given issue, taking on a mediating role among the various positions, including their own. Issues that could not be resolved at the sectoral tables were returned to the main table, where the neutral chair was able to provide the facilitation role required to resolve the outstanding issue, or present balanced advice to the CMIT for their consideration of the matter.

Overall, the internal-trade institutions were developed for a policy-making process governed by negotiation between governments. The tradition of executive federalism was expanded to include a neutral third party in the form of the chair of the table of chief negotiators, and a bureaucratic Internal Trade Secretariat dedicated specifically to one policy issue. In no small part, the success of the negotiations depended on this institutional design.

Framework Principles and Applications
The Agreement on Internal Trade finds its base in a set of principles and applications developed before the negotiations began. The principles agreed to were that

1 Governments treat people, goods, services and capital equally, irrespective of where they originate in Canada.
2 Governments reconcile standards and regulations to provide for the free movement of people, goods, services and capital within Canada.
3 Governments ensure that their administrative policies operate to pro-

vide for the free movement of people, goods, services and capital within Canada.

In applying these principles, governments recognize the need for

- full disclosure in information, legislation, regulations, policies and practices that have the potential to impede a single, integrated market in Canada;
- exceptions and transition periods as well as special needs consistent with regional development objectives in Canada;
- supporting administrative compliance mechanisms that are accessible, timely, credible and effective; and
- taking into account the importance of environmental objectives, consumer protection and labour standards (Committee of Ministers on Internal Trade 1992).

This framework of principles and applications represented the first comprehensive set of rules upon which the agreement would rest. Equally important, the framework provided the CMIT with a mandate to give to negotiators. And while the rules of the agreement were modified and expanded during the negotiations, the central thrust of the framework agreed to in December 1992 was maintained throughout the policymaking process.

Rules of Negotiation

The final hurdle that needed to be overcome before comprehensive internal-trade negotiations could begin was the development of a set of negotiating rules. The rules framework, agreed to by the CMIT on 18 March 1993, was designed with cooperation between jurisdictions in mind in their negotiations within the principles discussed above. Negotiations would begin no later than 1 July 1993 'to remove barriers and reconcile regulations, standards and administrative practices in all of the economic sectors and the subject areas agreed to by Governments.' The deadline for signing was agreed to be 30 June 1994. And, crucially, ministers agreed that an effective compliance mechanism was an essential component and would be part of the negotiations.

Thus, central to the rules of negotiation was setting a time-frame and deadline date as an impetus to complete the negotiations. With thirteen governments participating, it is not hard to imagine the logistical difficulties that could arise during a comprehensive negotiation process if no deadline was agreed to. Indeed, as many individuals associated with the negotiations have indicated to the authors, the very existence of time pressures proved to be a driving force in getting the deal done.

Another factor integral to the success of negotiations was the agreement to include some form of compliance or dispute-resolution mechanism. With the experience of negotiating the Canada–U.S. Free Trade Agreement (FTA) fresh in governments' minds, a compliance mechanism was understood to be vital for an internal agreement. Without such a mechanism any agreement would be toothless. Including compliance as an issue in the rules of negotiation not only guaranteed that such a mechanism would be developed, but also provided protection for those participants who were reluctant, fearing non-compliance, to negotiate more comprehensively.

Finally, the rules of negotiation further established the institutional order for internal-trade policy making by outlining the mandate of the CMIT as director of negotiations, while recognizing the ultimate authority of First Ministers. The role of the chief negotiators was formally established by the CMIT in June 1993.

Underlying this set of formal rules for the Agreement on Internal Trade was the implicit understanding that negotiations would follow a similar path to those of the General Agreement on Tariffs and Trade (GATT), FTA, and later NAFTA. In particular, the most-favoured-nation and national treatment provisions of GATT, and the importance of dispute-settlement procedures from the FTA, proved to be most influential in negotiating the Agreement on Internal Trade. The agreement institutes a 'most-favoured-province' provision whereby equivalent treatment for all Canadian persons, goods, services, and investments is established with respect to a 'best-in-Canada' measurement (Canada 1994, Article 401:3[a] and [b]), and a comprehensive provision for dispute resolution (Canada 1994, Part V). These provisos mirror those found in the GATT and FTA arrangements, and form a significant part of the backbone of the AIT. Indeed, it is clear that the experience with GATT and FTA not only had an impact on the structural aspects of the agreement, but also drove much of the philosophical and rules debate in the negotiations regarding the elimination of barriers to trade.

Key Negotiating Stages

The Pre–Federal Election Stage and Early Organizational Preparation

By the summer of 1993, all internal-trade institutions had been established, a set of guiding principles and applications mandated, and rules developed for the negotiating process. The negotiations were set to begin. However, also in the summer of 1993, a federal election was called by the then prime minister, Kim Campbell. With the possibility of a change in government looming, and the uncertainty about what effect such a change would have on the internal-trade policy process, negotiators and officials were reluctant to jump into full-fledged negotiations. As it turned out, the new Liberal government, represented at the CMIT by Industry Canada minister John Manley, continued along the path forged by its predecessor and fully supported the internal-trade agenda. Initial fears were thus unfounded.

Nonetheless, during the period between the institutionalization of the internal-trade issue and the 1993 federal election, the CMIT, the chief negotiators, and the Internal Trade Secretariat spent most of their time preparing for the negotiations. This interlude proved to be useful, as ministers and officials were able to complete as much background work as possible. This was an important stage, as many of the chief negotiators and their staffs were new to the internal-trade policy field and needed to be brought 'up to speed' prior to entering into the negotiations. The secretariat played a particularly important role during this time, and provided each jurisdiction with information regarding not only internal trade, but also all other Canadian trade initiatives. In essence, everybody was introduced to the Canadian trade lexicon.

Perhaps the most important work completed prior to the 1993 federal election (and shortly thereafter) had to do with beginning the process of developing the previously mentioned framework for internal trade, and establishing how to organize work on sectoral and other issues. Informed by the principles, applications, and rules of negotiation already set forth, a Working Group on Rules was established at the 13 July 1993 meeting of chief negotiators, chaired by Alberta and made up of Ontario, Canada, Quebec, New Brunswick, and British Columbia. On the basis of initial discussion papers presented by the Ontario and federal delegations, the working group was charged with the responsibility of looking at substantive issues regarding the affirmation of rights and responsibilities of provincial jurisdictions; the general obligations to be confirmed, including the concept of reciprocal non-discrimination; issues of market access; and the delineation of how binding the agreement should be.

Most of the initial discussion instituted by the Working Group on Rules centred on what rules should be established and how these should apply during sectoral negotiations. Of the options presented, it was ultimately agreed that a set of rules would be generally applicable; that rules developed by the sectoral tables and chapters would be guided by the general rules; and that, if sectoral negotiators deemed it necessary to deviate from the general rules, permission would be granted only by the table of chief negotiators.

In the discussion of specific rules, general agreement was quickly reached on the desirability of transparency and the reconciliation of governmental standards. However, with respect to the issues of no barriers to trade and standards for non-discrimination, differences arose. In particular, some provinces were concerned about their ability to promote regional-development policies. It was suggested by Ontario that provinces maintain the right to govern within a jurisdiction first, with any trade effects being considered secondary. The federal delegation was concerned that such a narrow idea of rules contravened the underlying philosophy of a comprehensive agreement. British Columbia and New Brunswick, on the other hand, were supportive of the identical-treatment idea, but were concerned that equality of treatment not be confused with fairness of treatment, and that careful attention be paid to areas where identical treatment might lead to *de facto* discrimination in some jurisdictions.

The interplay between jurisdictions with respect to rules continued into the fall of 1993. At the 1–2 September meeting of chief negotiators, a draft framework on rules was presented by Alberta. This framework called for several integral sections to be included – specifically, 'Introduction,' comprising 'preamble,' 'Objectives and Definitions,' and 'Reaffirmation of Constitutional Responsibilities'; 'General Obligations,' with articles dedicated to 'Non-Discrimination,' 'Entry and Exit,' 'Disguised Restrictions,' 'Reconciliation of Regulations and Standards-Related Measures,' and 'Transparency and Conformity,' and sections on 'Application of General Obligations to Sectors,' 'Institutional Arrangements' (administration and dispute-resolution mechanism), and 'Final Provisions.' While this draft framework represented the first comprehensive rules model, debate still continued – particularly with respect to how comprehensive the rules should be, and to what extent exemptions or qualifiers should be admitted during sectoral negotiations. Still, the Alberta recommendations proved to be valuable, as they focused the debate and allowed for further sub–working groups to complete analysis at a more micro level over the next two months. A finalized and revised 'Draft Framework for a Canadian Agreement on Internal Trade' was presented to the table of chief negotiators and the CMIT for their consideration on 5 November 1993.

This early work on developing the architecture for the Agreement on Internal Trade proved to be much more difficult than had been initially predicted by many officials. Indeed, the rules were not finally agreed to until early in 1994 (Committee of Ministers on Internal Trade, 20 January 1994). Yet, given the importance of having a firm set of ground rules upon which to negotiate the agreement, the efforts required to overcome difficulties appear to have been worthwhile. Without such a set of rules, it is plausible to suggest that no negotiations would have taken place. In fact, in the early stages of the policy-making process one of the few things about which there was unanimous agreement was the necessity of establishing an architectural framework before bargaining could begin.

Several important lessons emerged out of the process leading to the initial agreement on framework rules. In the first place, proof was finally evident that policy making by negotiation between jurisdictions could be successful. The negotiating institutions, specifically led by the neutral chair, showed that they could work, and this fact offered hope for the future negotiations. Second, the mandate given to the negotiators by their ministers also proved to be an effective one. With political pressure emanating from the CMIT, the table of chief negotiators and sub–working groups were forced to negotiate a rules framework that closely matched the spirit of an internal-trade policy presented at the ministerial level. Finally, the Internal Trade Secretariat realized that it had to play a strong, albeit impartial, role in forging the agreement. Taken together, the lessons from bargaining over the architecture of the agreement acted as a model for the substantive negotiations that were to follow.

January 1994 to April 1994: Securing a Mandate and Creating a Text

In early January 1994, the table of chief negotiators presented the CMIT with a mid-term report on the progress of the internal-trade negotiations. This report was considered in depth at the 19–20 January 1994 CMIT meeting in Ottawa. Much of the discussion, at the request of the chief negotiators, centred on the draft architecture of the agreement and on the debate over whether rules would be generally applicable or sector-specific. In addition, negotiators were interested in the CMIT reaffirming their mandate and gaining a more precise indication of ministerial priorities with respect to specific sectors.

The CMIT debate proved to be difficult, as consensus regarding the architecture of the agreement, and in particular its applicability, was not immediately achieved. However, ministers did agree that any rules framework should be as simple as possible to interpret and apply, and that the dispute-resolution mechanism should be equally easy to understand and use. It was unanimously determined that such a mechanism would avoid the involvement of the judicial system. In their final directions to negotiators, ministers confirmed the time-frame for completion of the negotiations, set forth a table of contents for an Agreement on Internal Trade, instructed the secretariat to prepare a draft text of the agreement by 14 February 1994, and asked the chief negotiators to present a preliminary text of an agreement to the CMIT by 31 March 1994 (Committee of Ministers on Internal Trade, 10 January 1994).

Preparation of a draft text for discussion and revision by the chief negotiators began shortly after the CMIT meeting. The goal of this exercise was to present a text that reflected, as much as possible, the views held by chief negotiators and sectoral tables. The draft was to be coherent and comprehensive, although it was implicitly understood that at such an early stage in the negotiations the text was unlikely to be acceptable in whole or in part to delegations. Still, the exercise proved to be invaluable. In large part, the practical effect that having a text had on the policy-making process was of benefit. A draft text enabled negotiators to focus their debate on specific provisions of the agreement – the implication being that modifications could be analysed, and the text added to or deleted from, in response to any new consensus. The draft basically set the agenda for the rest of the negotiating period.

In addition to the practical effect, the initial draft text also represented the first time that the political objectives of the CMIT and First Ministers had been put into a policy format. This was an important step in bringing the internal-trade issue out of the idea stage and into the policy world.

Finally, the preparation of the draft text further enhanced the Internal Trade Secretariat's role as a key institutional player. Charged with the responsibility for writing the text of the agreement, the secretariat assumed an impartial role in the further negotiating process. Able to play the part of a concerned neutral party, the secretariat used its administrative mandate to prod negotiators along. And while this bureaucratic pressure had no effect on the contents of the text, it did have considerable influence over its completion.

The stage was ultimately set for completing a deal in April 1994. At the CMIT meeting held in Ottawa on 7 April, ministers provided what amounted to a final set of directions for negotiating the agreement. Based on the precepts of maximizing coverage and minimizing exemptions, the CMIT directed the chief negotiators (and the secretariat) to prepare a second draft text by 2 May 1994 (Committee of Ministers on Internal Trade, 7 April 1994). It was this draft text that was debated during the end-game stage of negotiations in May and June 1994, and formed the framework of the finalized Agreement on Internal Trade.

The Institutions in Action

Prior to dealing with the actual dynamics in chapters 4 to 8, it is helpful to offer a further capsule profile of the institutions in action beyond that supplied in our initial descriptive portrait above.

First Ministers

The role of First Ministers in the actual negotiations of the Agreement on Internal Trade was limited. And although they were ultimately responsible for the signing of the agreement on 18 July 1994, First Ministers can be viewed as having played a more philosophical than practical role in the negotiations. This was not a minor role, however, as it was the political pressure and muscle from the top that forced both the CMIT and the negotiators to complete their work within the required time-frame. Furthermore, First Ministers developed the institutions of internal trade, and provided the necessary political environment in which these institutions could work successfully.

Committee of Ministers of Internal Trade (CMIT)

As has already been indicated, the CMIT was left to resolve the outstanding issues regarding exceptions within sectors to the general rules set out in the architecture of the agreement. The majority of this debate centred around jurisdictional powers – but in a slightly non-traditional way.

Typical in Canadian interjurisdictional policy making are debates between the federal and provincial governments over jurisdictional powers. Usually, this debate is couched in terms of one jurisdiction attempting to gain more power at the expense of the other. However, the internal-trade debates witnessed a dynamic in federal–provincial policy making whereby intrajurisdictional debate surfaced more frequently than would be the case in discussions focusing on a single policy field. Instead of argument being restricted to debate between jurisdictional levels, the internal-trade policy debate was shaped by interdepartmental struggle within provincial governments, and among provincial governments.

Whereas the federal government was interested in seeing the internal-trade policy from a national perspective, and tried to play a mediating role towards this end, it fully understood that in many of the chapters it had a small role to play – essentially leaving the debate up to the provinces. The provinces, on the other hand, were split into three general camps: those interested in maintaining their ability to govern freely within their jurisdiction, those with a strong desire for free internal trade, and those with a more mixed position. As we show in chapter 4, debate among these camps at the CMIT, especially in the end-game meetings on 22 and 27–28 June, shaped the final policy trade-offs reflected in the agreement (Committee of Ministers on Internal Trade, 28 June 1994).

Table of Chief Negotiators

The table of chief negotiators can be viewed as having more of a directive and brokerage role than sectoral tables. Still, it was the responsibility of the main table to set the practical agenda for negotiations, to act as mediator and conciliator (i.e., especially the neutral chair, whose role is discussed in chapter 4), and to focus the work of the sectoral tables within the context of the overall agreement.

During the final stages of the negotiations, the main table, with help from the secretariat, was responsible for developing the final draft text of the agreement for perusal by the CMIT. At this stage, though, things began to unravel, and many issues were left unresolved. Primarily the difficulty lay in exceptions within sectors. The provinces were interested in gaining as many exceptions as possible (mainly for regional-development reasons), while the federal government was interested in establishing a more general rules-based policy document. This disagreement was not resolved until the ministerial meetings in late June, and threatened the success of the negotiations. The neutral chair, although armed with the mandate to prevent such an eventuality, was only just able to keep the process moving forward. Eventually, it was the work of the main table in concert with the CMIT that resulted in the deal being forged.

Sectoral Tables

The majority of the provisions of Part IV of the agreement were negotiated at the sectoral tables. Jurisdictions who had a greater interest than others in a given sector were more likely to be a member of the sectoral table, and thus debate was often more specific at this level than at the main table. In addition, a smaller group facilitated more precise negotiations.

Perhaps the greatest influence that sectoral tables had on the final agreement had to do with the application (or lack thereof) of the general rules. As might be expected, negotiating dynamics within sectors often led to an application for exception within that sector to the general rules. Indeed, in all sectors, the specific rules do not identically match the general rules. The process of negotiating these exceptions, both internal to the sectoral table and with its external relationship to the main table and the CMIT, proved to be the biggest stumbling block of the entire negotiating process. In fact, exceptions were debated right up to the point at which the agreement was finalized.

The main reason for the difficulty associated with rules exception at the sectoral tables had to do with the issue of provincial power, especially as it related to regional development. As we will see in more detail in chapters 4 and 5, many provinces, notably British Columbia, Saskatchewan, and Nova Scotia, were worried that the general rules of the agreement – in particular, those related to reciprocal non-discrimination and no obstacles – detracted from their ability to institute economic-development policies within their jurisdiction. In most cases these issues were irresolvable at the sectoral level and had to be dealt with by the CMIT at the late June 1994 meetings. The effect that such policy stances had on the final agreement was not trivial, and has led some commentators to view it as part of the reason why the internal-trade document lacks sufficient 'bite' (Trebilcock and Schwanen 1995).

The Internal Trade Secretariat

The secretariat's main role in the early stages of the negotiation process was to provide analytical resources to other institutional players. This role was valuable in terms of establishing a common level of understanding about the internal-trade policy issue. During the final negotiations, however, the analytical role tended to be directed more to specific areas of debate. When negotiators at either the main table or sectoral tables had questions about the impact of a particular decision or the applicability of framework rules, the secretariat provided the necessary analysis.

Not surprisingly, one issue that received careful analytical attention was the 'constitutionality' of the agreement. From the outset, consensus existed that no agreement should abrogate jurisdictional powers defined in the constitution. As a result, the negotiations were especially cumbersome when jurisdictional power was in question (e.g., with respect to regional development). The secretariat thus had to ensure that any negotiated settlement in the internal-trade policy field had no constitutional effect. At times administering the negotiating process proved to be an extremely difficult job for the secretariat. Working closely with the chair, the secretariat was partly responsible for the successful completion of negotiations.

Conclusions

The internal-trade negotiations had a decade-long gestation period. From the mid-1980s until about 1990, the issue of internal trade could barely grab the lower rung of the priority-setting ladder. The early views of academics and the Macdonald Commission were not seized upon politically as a priority concern until further paradigm shifts in thinking and learning occurred. This involved initially the listing of the issue in a larger nexus of regional-development issues, and then a greater awareness as crucial new international-trade agreements were negotiated. It is also undoubtedly the case that the agenda for negotiation was given a special impetus by the failure of constitutional initiatives in the 1990s.

While this gestation process was under way, a necessary form of learning and institution-building was going on. This contributed a valuable training ground for the institutions that would be needed for the conduct of the negotiations, and for subsequent implementation of any agreement that might result. The prospect of the 1993 election also forced a useful hiatus and enabled some important preparatory work to be done, in particular allowing research to be undertaken and the system of negotiating tables to be worked out, and, in an overall sense, making it possible to think through the architecture of the agreement. The drafting of an initial text also was a crucial step towards the negotiations that truly began in the first six months of 1994.

The winding road to the actual negotiations by no means guaranteed success. Indeed, the journey suggested that the odds favoured failure. From the broadly descriptive account in this chapter, we now turn to an examination of the dynamics of the negotiations.

PART TWO:
THE NEGOTIATIONS AND MULTIPLE–POLICY
FIELD POLICY MAKING

4

The Core of the Agreement:
The Provinces and Negotiation Issues and Dynamics

There are three ways to tell the story of the internal-trade negotiations: a detailed chronological account, meeting by meeting, from start-up to the end-game; an issues-based approach; and a players–alliances approach. The focus of this chapter is on the last of these perspectives, but with necessary continuous references to the issues at stake. A detailed chronological treatment has not been attempted, in part because it would be too lengthy, but also because it is not necessary for the primary purposes of the analysis. There is, however, frequent reference in the analysis below to what provincial negotiators thought broadly of the early, middle, and end-game stages of the negotiations.

The chapter is primarily concerned with the positions and approaches taken by the provinces or clusters of provinces. These positions focus ultimately on the main end-game battles, which centred on a set of interlocked issues: procurement, regional and other key exceptions, legitimate objectives, and dispute settlement. We also comment further on how the federal government's negotiating approaches and positions evolved and were perceived.

We cannot tell the detailed story of all twelve jurisdictions in this book. The ten provinces are profiled here, but available space and actual negotiating dynamics require that clusters of provinces be examined, especially in the case of Atlantic Canada but with regard to other groupings as well. Thus Alberta and Manitoba are grouped as Conservative pro-free-trade allies of the federal government. Quebec, not for first time, needs discussion on its own but in the context of a crucial relationship with the federal government. The three provinces with NDP governments in 1994 – Ontario, British Columbia, and Saskatchewan – are grouped as an alliance of more sceptical participants, concerned mainly with governance

AUGUSTANA UNIVERSITY COLLEGE
LIBRARY

and legitimate objectives. Finally, the four Atlantic provinces (and the two territorial governments) are grouped as cautiously supportive of free trade but fearing abandonment by the larger provinces and by the federal government. As indicated in chapter 1, we are also interested in the way in which the provinces saw the negotiations in terms of their own underlying real economy; the relative weighting of internal-trade goals versus legitimate objectives in the context of federal–provincial relations; and concerns and visions of national unity. These issues in turn were often linked to partisan and ideological positions among clusters of NDP provincial governments.

In the last section of the chapter we examine briefly the role of Arthur Mauro, the Winnipeg lawyer and businessman who was appointed as the neutral chair of the central negotiating table. We also comment briefly on the role of the Ottawa-based Internal Trade Secretariat and on the general nature of the provincial approaches to coordinating negotiating teams.

Alberta and Manitoba as Pro-Free-Trade Allies

Alberta and Manitoba were undoubtedly the most supportive allies the federal government had in the AIT process. The Conservative governments in both provinces broadly continued their earlier pattern of support for international free trade, as exhibited in the NAFTA process. But there were, of course, differences in the more particular rationales and motivations, with Alberta being more ideological in its basic stance and Manitoba being more pragmatic, taking into account the underlying nature of its economy.

Alberta

Alberta's position in the negotiations was that it wanted as close to 100 per cent internal free trade as possible. If anything, it was a stronger advocate of a disciplined agreement than the federal government and was certainly Ottawa's most ardent ally. The Klein government, strongly in favour of free enterprise, entered the negotiations willing to give up Alberta's own remaining barriers. While it felt that Alberta did not have a great many of them, it did know that internal free trade could mean giving up some of its resource-related regulatory practices, such as removal permits and related instruments, that had in the past contributed to the building of the Alberta oil-and-gas and petrochemical industry.

From the outset, the Alberta negotiating approach was seen as a government-wide or corporate commitment, and its negotiators spoke for the government, a condition which Alberta's key people often thought did not obtain for other participating governments, including the federal government. Its chief negotiator was a trusted former provincial Cabinet minister, Jim Horsman, whose links with the premier were close. Interestingly, the negotiations were anchored in the Federal and Intergovernmental Affairs ministry rather than in the provincial Industry department, as was typically the case in other provincial governments.

Alberta's position favouring a strong internal-trade agreement was quite consistently applied across the various elements of the agreement. Thus, it supported a tough dispute-settlement process with wide opportunities for private (business) access, including the awarding of costs and damages. In this regard, and on the agreement in general, Alberta was one of the few provinces to directly and actively consult its business community during the negotiations. Most other provinces relied on their own departments' views of their business clientele.

Alberta also sought to ensure that the architecture of the agreement gave clear priority to the general rules and that exceptions were minimized. For example, in the end Alberta expressed the view that the 'legitimate objectives' section was too broad. It sought a wide and effective procurement agreement and strong limits on regional-development policies, provincial or federal. Indeed, Alberta explicitly referred to regional policy as social-welfare policy. Moreover, since it had few Crown corporations, it also sought to ensure that other provinces' Crown corporations were not being required by their governments to practise provincial development policy.

As the negotiations came to a crunch on the combined issues of procurement, investment, the Crowns, and regional development, Alberta sought to 'smoke out' its two NDP-governed neighbouring provinces. Saskatchewan and British Columbia favoured more exceptions in each of the issues noted above, but Alberta was concerned that it would bear the brunt of such policies. In other words, investment and economic activity might be attracted to its immediate neighbours, Saskatchewan and British Columbia, rather than to Alberta. As a consequence, Alberta insisted on and obtained provisions which allowed a process of retaliation (Article 1710). In B.C. and Saskatchewan, NDP governments had campaigned electorally on their intention to use these tools of economic development.

Alberta, however, did temper its retaliation clause somewhat out of a sensitivity for Quebec's situation (described below). On a wider federalism front, Alberta saw Quebec as a consistent ally and recognized the sensitivities Quebec faced. Accordingly, the retaliation provisions were such that they would be phased-in a year after the agreement took effect.

Alberta's negotiators also saw the labour mobility, transportation, and agricultural and food goods chapters as positive developments, and good reasons for signing on. Alberta was not concerned that there was no energy chapter. Alberta believed that an energy chapter ought to cover all energy forms, including electricity, but since that was not possible, it was better, in Alberta's view, not to have a chapter at all. In practice, there was virtual internal free trade in oil and gas in any event.

The positions that Alberta took should not be viewed as an indication that the province had no concerns about legitimate objectives and provincial powers. Alberta defended the position that constitutional powers could not be changed by the agreement, but it tended in a broader sense to seek what it referred to as 'policy flexibility.' Alberta also took the lead in securing a provision in the agreement that would require greater provincial consultation than in the past in *international*-trade negotiations (Article 1809.4) The logic here was that, if the tentacles of international-trade agreements were extending into provincial domains, then provincial roles had to extend into the negotiation of trade agreements by the federal government. This provision for consultation by the provinces in international-trade negotiations was reluctantly agreed to by the federal government.

Manitoba

The Conservative government of Manitoba, headed by Premier Gary Filmon, was a broadly supportive of the need for a good internal-trade agreement. Support for such an agreement was non-partisan in nature in that the former NDP provincial government had supported the early efforts in the 1980s and was also a supporter of the Canada–U.S. Free Trade Agreement.

The Manitoba view flowed in part from the nature of the province's economy, which depended on internal trade. Centred on east–west transportation and service industries, the Manitoba economy was neither as resources-dependent as Saskatchewan's or Alberta's nor as industrial as Ontario's. Its gateway form of economy had for most of the post–Second World War period been characterized by fairly stable development. Neither its booms nor its low points were as great as in its neighbouring provinces.

The Filmon government and its small team of negotiators in the Department of Industry and Tourism also entered the negotiations with the view that Manitoba had few barriers to discard and few irritants that could be attributed to other provincial or federal policies and practices. Its goal was simply to get a good, effective deal.

This posture of support, and of, in a sense, being above the battle, was also reinforced by the fact that two of Manitoba's lead ministers, Eric Stephanson and Jim Downey (the deputy premier), were also, in turn, the co-chairs of the negotiations, along with federal industry minister John Manley. The adoption of a helpful fixer role was also affected by the fact that the key facilitator in the negotiations, Arthur Mauro, was a political confrère of Premier Gary Filmon's, and was, moreover, based in Winnipeg throughout the negotiations.

On specific issues, Manitoba was among the stronger supporters of dispute-settlement provisions that would include significant private access. This position did not come from any groundswell of expressed support from the Manitoba business community. In fact, the Manitoba negotiators did not launch any special consultation process with provincial business interests. Indeed in some respects Arthur Mauro, as a Manitoba businessman-lawyer, was seen as a partial surrogate business voice. Manitoba's negotiators of course knew that Mauro was a neutral facilitator, and hence not their representative, but his presence was a form of additional reassurance.

Canada's middle province shared some concerns about preserving some room for regional policy and legitimate objectives, but, far more than others, it was prepared to see these always hedged in by rules and requirements for transparency. In the end, Manitoba signed on the dotted line believing that the agreement was a significant step forward. Perhaps in part as a result of Manitoba's supportive role and location in the centre of the country, the Internal Trade Secretariat established under the agreement is based in Winnipeg and is currently gearing up for its permanent role under the Agreement on Internal Trade.

Quebec and the Political Need for an Economic Union

As the internal-trade negotiations proceeded, the Quebec Liberal government and its negotiators could not help but be aware that an election would be held in 1994. Indeed, it is undoubtedly the case that it was the election itself and the potential for a victory by the Parti Québécois that provided the ultimate leverage of the negotiations – a firm deadline. No negotiation can progress very successfully without a real deadline. In the FTA, NAFTA, and GATT negotiations, these deadlines/disciplines were in essence supplied by the U.S. fast-track trade-policy-making rules (Hart 1994; Doern and Tomlin 1991a). For the Canadian internal-trade negotiations, the initial muscle for a deadline had been supplied by federal trade minister, Michael Wilson, in concert with Prime Minister Brian Mulroney and the premiers. The June 1994 deadline is largely a testament to their ability to get First Ministers to agree. The deadline had been devised with the awareness that there would be a Quebec election, although the exact date could not be known. As the negotiations proceeded, however, the looming Quebec election concentrated the negotiators' attention.

The goals of the Quebec government were undoubtedly delicately balanced between a desire to show that progress could be made in federal–provincial matters following the dual 1990s defeats of the Meech Lake and the Charlottetown accords, and a determination to demonstrate the openness of the Quebec economy in the Canadian economic union. At the same time Quebec had to demonstrate to voters that it was not ceding powers to the federal government.

The desire to show federal–provincial progress meant that Quebec approached the negotiations in an extremely serious but low-profile manner. It did not want the negotiations to fail, because it was important to be able to demonstrate to potential swing voters that change was possible within federalism. It had an important stake in advancing the four freedoms of an economic union because, in the wake of the constitutional failures, the Bourassa government, including Premier Bourassa himself, had frequently referred to the European Union as a potential model for a new Quebec–Canada accommodation within federalism (Quebec 1991; Quebec Liberal Party 1991; Doern 1991). The Parti Québécois, within its sovereigntist option, was also speaking of the firm need for an economic union with Canada. The Bourassa government had also been a strong supporter of the FTA and NAFTA, and hence the thrust of a liberalized market approach was clear in Quebec's overall economic posture (Gagnon 1993).

However, an economic union in general was not the same as an economic union with specifics. Thus, when it came to determining exactly what economic union actually meant, Quebec was meticulously careful about what could be agreed to, and be seen to be agreed to, in the run-up to an election. Other provinces knew this as well and played it to their own advantage in general alliance formation and on details. Thus, on the issue of having broad legitimate objectives, and minimal dispute-settlement provisions, Quebec and the NDP provinces found considerable common cause with Saskatchewan and B.C. Some common cause was also found with the Atlantic provinces over the issue of regional-policy exemptions.

As always, Quebec and Ontario knew concretely about the vital importance of interprovincial trade between the two jurisdictions. The procurement agreement between the two provinces (see more below) brokered late in 1993 was an important breakthrough and 'trust-builder.' Quebec's trade minister, Gerard Tremblay, and its chief negotiator, Daniel Baudet, had been closely involved with Frances Lankin and the Ontario negotiators. Ontario and Quebec also cooperated over the delicate issue of Crown corporations. Of crucial practical and symbolic importance in this regard were the concerns about Hydro-Québec and Ontario Hydro. The internal-trade agreement's delicately crafted provisions, disciplines, and timing provisions on the Crown corporations were designed to allow the Quebec Liberal government to defend themselves. Quebec legislation on Hydro-Québec still explicitly provided for an economic-development role and could not be changed quickly. At the same time, the Quebec government knew that GATT–WTO and NAFTA provisions were moving in similar directions, and thus new rules were coming one way or another.

The fact that there was no energy chapter in the agreement can in some respects also be attributed in part to Quebec's insistence, but with support coming from Ontario and New Brunswick. The dispute here was primarily between Newfoundland and Quebec, and centred on the issue of the cross-provincial boundary movement, or 'wheeling,' of electricity (Canada 1988). Newfoundland wanted to be able to wheel electricity across Quebec for export elsewhere. But this view was tied to past low-price contracts which Quebec was benefiting from in its earlier deals with Newfoundland over Labrador power exports to Quebec. In a larger sense, however, the absence of an energy chapter was the result of a number of factors linked to rapidly changing aspects of the electricity industry and of key provincial Crown corporations. The oil-and-gas aspects of internal trade in energy were not an obstacle, but, as indicated above, Alberta was opposed to a full energy chapter unless all modes of energy were included. Moreover, each province and its electrical utility were facing different combinations of concerns about possible privatization, huge sunk costs, and partial competition in the industry made possible by technology.

Quebec was also tenacious in the end-game about culture and cultural industries being exempt from the AIT, along with financial services and matters of taxation. In agricultural matters, it was crucial for Quebec, politically and otherwise, that marketing boards and supply management not be included. It only reluctantly agreed to the incentives code in the investment chapter.

The NDP Provinces: Variously Sceptical Free-Trade Critics

The NDP-governed provinces of Ontario, B.C., and Saskatchewan suggest a natural grouping in that they could be expected to be staunch defenders of the legitimate objectives of the provinces as governing entities in a federation. Moreover, the three provinces had each exhibited a strong scepticism about the earlier international free-trade negotiation processes and were accordingly suspicious of what the federal government might be up to in its AIT initiative. But, as always in federal–provincial and interprovincial politics, the common denominator of partisanship can be taken only so far. The three NDP provinces turned out to be variously sceptical.

Ontario

The government of Ontario headed by Premier Bob Rae entered the internal-trade negotiation process in a cautious and reluctant manner. The NDP government members, in particular its core labour-union supporters, were against the recently completed North American Free Trade Agreement and regarded the internal-trade negotiations as a federal trap (Abelson and Lusztig 1996). On the other hand, the Ontario economy profited enormously from the internal-trade market. Ontario had a negative foreign-trade balance but a hugely positive internal-trade balance. With respect to the size and extent of the remaining barriers within the internal market, Ontario's internal-trade negotiating team was extremely sceptical about the business community's claims that remaining barriers were costing the Canadian economy up to $6 billion in economic activity.

On the national-unity front, however, Ontario was aware that, following the failure of the Charlottetown Accord, and given a Quebec election in the near future, federalism had to be shown to work in an effort to confront discord in Quebec. In short, a deal had to be concluded successfully. Ontario's view of what a successful deal might look like, however, was also conditioned by a sense that the negotiation might indeed fail. Accordingly, it would have been satisfied to see a smaller sign of progress, based on dealing with barriers on a 'sector by sector' basis. It saw any internal-trade agreement as being organic in that it would be gradually built upon later. In this sense it saw any deal reached as an evolving political agreement.

Ontario also based its negotiating strategy on a view that almost any gain by other provinces would be at Ontario's expense. It therefore placed emphasis on the principle of *reciprocal non-discrimination*, in effect saying that, if other provinces did not discriminate against Ontario, Ontario would not discriminate against them. In a related sense, Ontario was 'the United States' of Canada, the market everybody else wanted access to. At the same time, there was a concern in the Ontario camp that, far from reducing barriers, an agreement might freeze the status quo and entrench current 'protectionist' practices.

For Ontario, as for several other provinces, the issue of procurement was central to the deal but always paired with regional-development exceptions. In the fall of 1993, Ontario became embroiled in a long-festering dispute with Quebec on public-procurement matters and on labour-mobility issues. The dispute became front-page news. Indeed, in both Ontario and Quebec, the elevation of the dispute into a media event was seen as a necessary step in gaining leverage on the issue, especially within Quebec. As noted above, Quebec was anxious to show that it did indeed support the concept of an economic union. In any event, these disputes led to the signing of a December 1993 agreement between Ontario and Quebec on the 'Opening of Procurement for Ontario and Quebec.' For Ontario, this approach was seen as an example of the value of sector-by-sector problem solving, but it also helped clear the decks for the later June 1994 deal on internal trade.

Procurement barriers were seen in Ontario as important but also problematical, primarily because of the perceived institutional differences of the Ontario and Quebec procurement regimes. Quebec's approach was much more rule-based and, in this sense, transparent and more centralized. Ontario's procurement system, particularly as it extended down into the local government, hospital, and education sectors, had evolved into a series of informal practices for which there was, in many areas, not even a credible information base or paper trail.

In the end-game of the negotiations, when some provinces sought a maximum set of regional-policy exemptions, Ontario led the counter-thrust to ensure that exemptions were limited and that for each exemption there would be a corresponding set of restraining and reporting disciplines to limit the use made of the exemption. Again, this was because Ontario saw regional policies as being essentially losses for Ontario.

Ontario was also the key player in advancing the doctrine of the 'non-intervention commitment' by governments in the behaviour of Crown corporations (Annex 520.2B). Ontario's NDP government had its own sympathy for the policy role of Crown corporations, but, at the same time, particularly with regard to Quebec, it sought restrictions. Ontario recognized it was often difficult to stop Crown corporations themselves from doing certain things that happened to favour local suppliers (Ontario had these problems too), but it wanted to ensure that governments would not themselves engage in or require discriminatory practices. The idea of the non-intervention commitment was adapted from the then ongoing GATT–WTO negotiations, during which similar problems arose among nations and their state enterprises.

In essence, Ontario seemed to adopt with its internal trading partners a 'show us' approach. On the reciprocal non-discrimination front, in the regional-policy disciplines, and in the 'non-intervention commitment' doctrines, Ontario wanted to be shown in a transparent way that whatever else other provinces might be doing to promote their economies, those measures were actually working and were not harming Ontario.

Ontario's positions often found some common cause with fellow NDP governments in Saskatchewan and B.C. Some of this was reflected in the stout defence of the 'legitimate objectives' parts of the agreement. Ontario, especially through its lead minister, Frances Lankin, shared in the general concern that provincial governments preserve their basic public-interest powers and capacities. But such alliances of philosophy could be carried only so far among the three NDP-governed provinces. Interestingly, the dynamics of negotiation were also aided by the fact that Lankin had herself been a public-service-union negotiator, and hence had good instincts about negotiation. Many other delegations have given her considerable credit for her problem-solving and negotiating skills and recognized that her hard work was one of the keys to the success of the deal.

British Columbia

If Alberta was the most avid supporter of an internal-trade agreement, then British Columbia was its most combative sceptical opponent, both among the NDP grouping and among the provinces as a whole. B.C.'s NDP premier, Mike Harcourt, eventually signed on, but there is virtual unanimity among other provinces that B.C. was the most overtly hostile to the process, from the early days to the end-game. B.C. was suspicious that, in the wake of constitutional failure, the AIT was a deal being cooked up by the federal Liberal government both to weaken provincial powers and to play out a Quebec-centred strategy.

With its NDP government, B.C. shared some of the basic philosophical opposition to the federal government's free-trade agenda and saw the proposed internal-trade agenda as an extension of it and as an attempt to weaken provincial governments. It also objected during the negotiations when, periodically, Quebec would use European Union institutional models as preferred ways of proceeding. For B.C., there was a strong aversion to thinking of Canada's provinces in international-trade terms, as an implied set of surrogate nation-states.

There was also a disposition in the B.C. approach to prefer reasonable amounts of government intervention in the economy. Such issues were always somewhat more sharply defined in B.C. in that its provincial politics had for many decades been more polarized along left–right lines. While these differences had undoubtedly narrowed in the 1990s, they were still a factor, and indeed were an issue in the election that ended in a Harcourt victory. Aligned to this disposition was the B.C. government's tendency to not see the economic union as being disembodied from the social union, and from social policies.

Some of the combativeness of the B.C. position was also a product of the fact that its lead minister, both internally and on the Committee of Ministers of Internal Trade (CMIT), was Glen Clark (thereafter to be elected premier of B.C.). Clark had entered politics after a career in public-sector unionism and thus, in terms of both personality and position, was predisposed to be sceptical, even obstinate, about the process that was under way.

Undoubtedly another crucial factor in the B.C. position was its view of the basic nature of the province's economy. The province's trading patterns were clearly becoming increasingly oriented towards the Pacific Rim region, extending from the northwestern United States to Japan and the fast-growing Asian economies (Canada West Foundation 1996). In this sense there was only a limited disposition to be concerned about pan-Canadian trade. Moreover, if it had concerns about the internal market and policies affecting B.C., it was more likely to see federal policies as the culprit, such as those related to the fisheries.

B.C.'s early views about internal trade were based, somewhat like those of Ontario, on the strategic position that it would be better to deal with particular irritants than to have a wholesale negotiation. Once in the negotiating mode, B.C. participated fully, but, as stated above, in an extremely sceptical fashion. Its negotiators were knowledgeable and experienced, but it was felt by other negotiating teams that they also tended to go beyond what their political masters would, in the end, tolerate.

B.C.'s negotiators were also very sceptical of the inherent notion that all barriers were promoters of economic inefficiencies. They also simply did not believe that the claims of dynamic losses being made by the central Canada business lobby were at all proven in any analytically convincing manner. For this and other reasons, the province's views clearly were in the camp that wanted maximum exceptions and minimum rules. B.C. was especially determined to ensure that the procurement provisions contained no, or few, incursions into its local government, hospital, and education sectors. It staunchly opposed a dispute-settlement process with any teeth.

On the other hand, perhaps not surprisingly, B.C. was a supporter of the need for a reasonably good environment chapter. B.C. has a strong environmental movement in its provincial political scene, in part because of green forestry politics, not to mention fishery conservation, and thus it did not see this chapter as a concessionary 'add on,' as some provinces did. B.C. was also interested in an acceptable agricultural and food goods chapter, albeit one that was not too radical but would facilitate future progress.

Arguably the key for B.C. was the investment chapter. Had there not been some kind of an investment code of conduct that it could politically point to as a selling point, it is unlikely that B.C. would have signed the agreement. As a major location for incoming investment, B.C. was concerned, like Ontario, that other provinces could entice investment that would otherwise 'naturally' come to it. Some of these investment issues for B.C. had an immediate test case just as the deal was being signed – in the form of the United Parcel Service (UPS) (see chapter 8) moving three separate customer-service offices from B.C. and Ontario to New Brunswick, enticed there by the incentives and policies of the government of New Brunswick.

In the end-game, B.C. along with Newfoundland, played a hand that saw the exceptions list growing and the principles list narrowing. Only final pressure from the federal government, Ontario, and Saskatchewan dissuaded B.C. from walking away from a process it was unenthusiastic about from the start.

Saskatchewan

Saskatchewan, with an NDP government led by Premier Roy Romanow, was arguably the province that adopted a philosophical and negotiating position in the most tension with a trade perspective, for the simple reason that it saw the deal as much more than a trade pact. The province was concerned about governing powers and about social consequences, and entered the discussions with a strong scepticism about the underlying motives of the federal government. The Saskatchewan position was very much couched in terms of memories of past constitutional battles. For Premier Romanow and his internal-trade negotiators (mainly veterans of these same federal–provincial battles), these earlier disputes ranged from the resource-jurisdiction issues of the 1970s, the 1981 constitutional patriation, Meech Lake, and the just-completed and unhappy Charlottetown Accord adventure. In several of these instances, the federal government had sought to strengthen and assert its trade-and-commerce powers but had been beaten back.

The Saskatchewan negotiators did not see the provincial position as protectionist, but it was very cautious and careful because it did see the essence of the negotiations as that of reducing the exercise of provincial powers. Moreover, given the province's still largely resource-based economy, the NDP government did not see a lot that they would get out of the agreement. Like Ontario, it was also very sceptical of the central Canadian business community's claims about GNP losses in the order of $6 billion resulting from trade barriers.

Despite these strong sceptical positions, the Saskatchewan negotiating team did not initially, in 1993, get very strong political direction. They were in effect told to 'motor on.' The team also felt that it and other governments had surprisingly little reliable economic analysis and data to go on. In contrast, it had numerous background papers on the federal–provincial aspects of the many separate policy fields up for negotiation in the overall process.

By 1994, however, the negotiating mandates were crystallized. Saskatchewan's overall position was basically to keep the general rules to a minimum, maximize the exceptions, and keep dispute settlement to a minimum as well. More specifically, four kinds of concerns were flagged: the need to preserve the policy role of Crown corporations (an issue with inevitable links to procurement); the need to preserve reasonable regional-economic-development instruments; the avoidance of specific kinds of collateral damage to the Saskatchewan economy from other aspects of any final agreement; and the need to challenge the 'Ottawa mindset.' In Saskatchewan's view, this 'mindset' featured two dangerous tendencies: first, the tendency to see everything as trade, and hence to downplay the normal use of a province's right to govern; and, second, the tendency at times to see even natural economic differences and assets as being inherently a barrier.

The Saskatchewan approach was therefore, in part, educative, regarding the proper role of government and the necessity for a province to have some appropriate spending and regulatory powers to positively influence its provincial economy. It tried to show that these views were not just a replay of the traditional earlier NDP mindset of the Douglas–Blakeney eras, when provincial coffers were more plentiful, but that some tools were still needed, even in times of diminished budgets, and that such needs should be respected in a complex federation. Saskatchewan also sought to deflect attention towards the federal government's own barriers, including procurement policies.

The alliances with other provinces that Saskatchewan sought flowed in varying combinations from these areas of priority. It did see itself as philosophically in agreement with Ontario and B.C., the other two NDP-governed provinces. With Quebec it sought support for issues concerning the role of Crown corporations. With Atlantic Canada came common ground on regional-development powers. It had little agreement with Alberta, but even so it joined with Alberta to force the issue in Clause 1809.4, which secured a greater right for the provinces to be consulted in future international-trade negotiations.

Among the more particular provisions and issues that were pushed by Saskatchewan was that of aboriginal peoples. Saskatchewan wanted to avoid any potential later problems that might arise regarding negotiations over aboriginal self-government, or existing or treaty rights. Saskatchewan pointed out that aboriginal peoples had no representation in the negotiations. The result of this pressure was that Article 1802 was included, essentially creating an exemption so that nothing in the agreement applied to any measure adopted or maintained with respect to aboriginal peoples.

With respect to the role of interest groups, three final points about Saskatchewan as negotiator should be noted. First, as was the case for some other provinces, the province experienced very limited pressure from, or involvement by, its business community. Second, organized labour was not actively involved. Had they been, it would have been much more difficult for Saskatchewan's negotiators to agree to some matters in the AIT. Third, on environmental matters, the negotiators tactically decided that they did not want to take on the environmental groups. Hence, they were quite happy to see this chapter negotiated on its own. Moreover, the negotiating team was itself extremely small and understaffed, and, because of these resource constraints, simply had to deal with the top-priority items. In the end, Saskatchewan signed a deal that had some of the cautionary provisions it sought, but it did not sign with much enthusiasm.

Atlantic Canada and the Territories: Fearing Abandonment while Pursuing More Open Markets

It is difficult but necessary to deal with the four provinces of Atlantic Canada and the two territorial governments as a group. As we will see, the veiws of each on particular aspects of internal trade differed from the others', but nonetheless they shared many overall concerns about their more vulnerable economic situation. Underlying these was a fear of abandonment, by which is meant a concern that both the federal government and the other big provinces, especially Ontario and Quebec, would use the negotiations to bring to an end any commitment to regional policy and to the real capacity of such jurisdictions to attract investment and foster employment. On the other hand, the *realpolitik* and the underlying economy of the individual Atlantic provinces varied considerably.

Inevitably, as the largest of the Atlantic provinces Nova Scotia took the lead in those aspects where an Atlantic Canada strategy could be said to have been forged, such as on regional economic development. In the end-game phase, however, Newfoundland took a much harder-line stance than Nova Scotia when it sought to hold out for a massive list of exemptions from the general rules. The four provinces did caucus frequently, largely out the deeper concern about abandonment and, much like Saskatchewan, out of a distrust of federal government intentions after the Charlottetown Accord referendum defeat.

Nova Scotia

Nova Scotia approached the negotiations as a form of damage control, seeing itself as caught between a rock and a hard place, with the former being the federal government, and the latter the big provinces. Interestingly, this perception is confirmed in a symbolic sense because, in our interviews with officials in other provinces, the Atlantic provinces were literally described in the short-hand terminology, the lingo of negotiating as it were, as 'client states' of the federal government.

This highly dependent and defensive posture of course gave rise to companion strategies. There was some necessary willingness in Nova Scotia to 'go with the flow' and get some kind of an internal-trade deal, provided the province did not get clobbered in the process. Second, there were particular issues and irritants that Nova Scotia had in areas such as transportation and the fishery.

However, above all, the central Nova Scotia concern was that regional-development powers would be emasculated and, just as important, that the federal government would abandon its funding of regional incentive programs. As chapters 2 and 3 showed, federal industrial policy was already leaning in this direction and, as noted above, other provinces such as Alberta and Ontario did want such policies either ended or severely constrained. If both of the above events occurred, Nova Scotia's government would have to assume wider obligations (including for welfare) that were not at all fully appreciated in Ottawa, Toronto, or Quebec City.

Nova Scotia's mistrust of the internal-trade negotiation process was further fuelled by what its negotiators perceived as the federal government's not playing an honest broker role. Somehow there was an expectation that the federal government would be 'above the battle' rather than in it. Nova Scotia and other Atlantic Canada and territorial government participants also saw Ontario and British Columbia as being far too tactically and frequently obstructionist. Quebec was seen as being quiet and cautious, but making numerous behind-the-scenes deals with the federal government. All three of these larger provinces were seen by Nova Scotia as having few compunctions about applying political muscle to a politically weaker province.

The crucial regional-development issues were part of the end-game negotiations, and in these final stages it would appear that Nova Scotia and Newfoundland together coordinated the playing of their final hand. Newfoundland in effect became the aggressor, laying out what others saw as an almost ludicrously long list of exemptions. Nova Scotia played the middle game by presenting a more reasonable list. In the end, the Atlantic provinces found allies on the regional question from Saskatchewan and from the government of the Northwest Territories.

On issues such as procurement, all of the Atlantic provinces wanted room for use of local industrial benefits. Here they had more allies among the other provinces, but, in each case where room for manoeuvre was granted, it was almost always immediately constrained by the requirement for transparency and reporting, or for limits on the frequency of use.

In many other areas of the agreement, the Atlantic provinces had overall common cause with the final version of the agreement. On labour-mobility issues, Atlantic Canada was broadly supportive, provided there was some built-in way to give some consideration to high-local-unemployment situations such as in the fishery. On dispute settlement, Atlantic Canada supported constrained private-access rights for business, in part out of a fear that the federal government itself might arrange or support the launching of such cases/complaints. On investment issues, there was successful opposition, in league with others, to the excessive international trade–like language that the federal government was seeking to implant in the agreement. Atlantic Canada also sought limits to the free flow of investment capital, in that Nova Scotia had just privatized its electric utilities but insisted that shares be sold exclusively to Nova Scotia buyers.

New Brunswick

New Brunswick's goals and strategies for the negotiations were premised on its negotiators' view that the province had always had an open trading history and that this had been recently reinforced by New Brunswick activism in promoting various Atlantic Canada accords on procurement and on greater regional integration. Within the region, it saw itself as much more open than Nova Scotia.

The province's goal was to seek a reasonable expansion of internal trade, but in a way that reflected fair-trade opportunities. New Brunswick entered the negotiations with considerable frustration that some of the key issues had not been settled in previous *constitutional* negotiations. But, at the same time, once negotiations had begun there was a considerable concerted effort in the New Brunswick approach. This came first from the fact that Premier Frank McKenna was personally identified with a belief that traditional regional-policy approaches were no longer viable and that a province like New Brunswick simply had to, and could, compete. The centrepiece of that view was a provincial economic-development policy that was linking the service sector with provincial incentives and the provincial telecommunications industry centred in NBTel. The premier himself was undoubtedly the lead salesman for this aggressive effort to attract business, to a far greater extent than any other provincial premier was to a particular 'industrial policy.'

Another important link for the New Brunswick strategy arose from the fact that its chief negotiator was a long-time official who knew everything, including the detailed financial aspects, about the province's economic-development incentives and activities, virtually on a firm-by-firm basis. As

a result, New Brunswick was especially careful and aggressive in the negotiations regarding regional development and economic development, on
the one hand, and the investment chapter and its incentives code, on the
other. It lost no opportunity to point out to the federal government that
Ottawa was not alone in pursuing a 'jobs, jobs, jobs' strategy. Provincial
governments had to be able to do so too. And when Ontario negotiators
announced that Ontario would not send transfer payments to New Brunswick just so that New Brunswick could 'pick our pockets,' New Brunswick
reminded Ontario of its own vulnerability. Ontario was reminded that
U.S. cities like Buffalo, New York, were already, after free trade, enticing
Ontario jobs southward with similar policies to that of New Brunswick,
with nary a whimper from Ontario.

Prince Edward Island

As Canada's smallest province, Prince Edward Island took a quite pragmatic and selective view of the AIT negotiations. In part this arose out of
the fact that it basically had only one person directly involved in the negotiations, and hence picking key areas was a practical as well as tactical
necessity. P.E.I. saw itself as a small open economy. Agriculture and tourism were key industries, but the province viewed their future development as hampered by the considerable reduction of federal transfer
payments.

In both agriculture and tourism, particular issues were central in a way
in which they were not in other provinces. P.E.I. agriculture exhibited far
less dependence on supply management than did agriculture in other
provinces, and it had a greater concern with exports. Central to the agricultural economy was of course the potato industry, where one-third of
Canada's crop and sales came from. And within this sector there were
particular concerns about regulatory product standards for small pota-
toes, a growing gourmet-meal and specialized-product market where
trade barriers (foreign and domestic) were being erected.

On the tourism side, there were concerns in P.E.I. both about being an
open economy to promote incoming tourist trade and about historic
views of non-island ownership and control of land. These latter concerns
were tied to the investment negotiations of the AIT. In the distant past,
ownership issues were linked to the expulsion of the Acadians, and the
abuses of absentee landlords. In more recent historical terms, the land
issue centred on the fact that in P.E.I. less than 10 per cent of this land is
Crown-owned. Indeed, huge swathes of land are owned by forestry com-

panies. In the 1970s, concerns rose when large numbers of Ontario citizens bought land, often on a speculative basis. All of these concerns led to the passage of the Land Protection Act, which limited how much land could be owned by those not resident in P.E.I. A key issue for P.E.I. was to preserve these provisions as an exception in the investment chapter.

Newfoundland

As suggested above, Newfoundland's position in the AIT negotiations was at times almost as combative as British Columbia's. However, in a larger sense the government headed by Premier Clyde Wells had in the early 1990s already set itself in the direction of a freer trade–oriented economic-development strategy. Manufacturing was only about 4 per cent of the province's GDP, and provincial policy was aimed at doubling this to make the Newfoundland economy less overwhelmingly resource-dependent. Initially it saw this strategy in terms of three concentric circles, with the first being an open Atlantic Canada market; the second, an open Canadian market; and, the third, international markets. In fact, the Newfoundland view was that greater progress had been made internationally and in Atlantic Canada, and that the internal Canadian market was lagging the most.

The Newfoundland negotiators saw the province as an important exporter not only in aspects of the fishery and energy, but also in the energy-related professional-services sector. At the same time the local fishery was in a state of crisis due to overfishing and declining fish stocks, and hence Newfoundland was extremely concerned about its ability to implement policies, procurement and others, that would favour locally unemployed persons. Premier Wells had indicated to his negotiators that he wanted room to be able to use 'soft side' assistance measures and to practise industrial-benefit policies on resource projects. It was already apparent to the province that larger-scale subsidization was not possible simply because of fiscal realities.

In part because of its energy and related professional service-sector strengths, Newfoundland sought an open procurement chapter in particular and was disappointed by the extent of the exceptions in that chapter. On the other hand, as chapter 7 shows, it played it tough on energy matters regarding the 'wheeling' of electricity across provincial boundaries. Its long-standing dispute with Quebec meant that an energy chapter failed to emerge. Newfoundland also used the negotiations to press Quebec on labour-mobility issues and to foster greater mobility of labour in the agreement as a whole. During the negotiations, Quebec agreed to sign a deal on labour mobility, outside the AIT itself, which would be similar to that between Ontario and Quebec.

Finally, Newfoundland was among the more adamant provinces regarding the need for consensus-based, non-legal dispute-resolution processes and limited private-access. It wanted nothing to do with cash penalties, not only because it was a poor province, but also because it was certain that any such cases involving cash penalties payable by an offending province would inevitably end up in court. Had there been wide private-access provisions, Newfoundland, along with other provinces, would have insisted, as a condition of signing, that the scope of the agreement be greatly reduced.

Arthur Mauro and the Internal Trade Secretariat

The role of Arthur Mauro and of the Ottawa-based Internal Trade Secretariat was also crucial to the 1993–4 negotiating process. Mauro is a respected and experienced lawyer-businessman from Winnipeg who had been chief executive officer of a regional airline company, chair of a royal commission on transportation, chancellor of the University of Manitoba, and a legal practitioner whose work frequently involved arbitrating disputes. Politically he was a nationally well-connected Progressive Conservative but was not seen as a partisan party man. He was approached in June 1993 by the federal Minister of Industry and Trade, Michael Wilson, and the Manitoba co-chair, Eric Stephanson. They advised Mauro that they were concerned that, if the negotiations were left simply to the chief negotiators, success would be in jeopardy. There had to be a neutral chair/facilitator.

Mauro agreed to take on the job after he was told that his name had received unanimous support from all ministers and governments involved. There were some concerns expressed about whether his French-language skills were good enough (a concern which Mauro had as well), but these worries were not a major obstacle.

Mauro took up his post knowing full well that the potential existed for the politics to be explosive, particularly as a consequence of the sense in some provinces after the failed Meech Lake and Charlottetown accords that the federal government was up to 'another' of its exercises. Like any mediator/facilitator, Mauro had to quickly determine what the basic alignment of forces and interests was. He then had to reduce the issues to the crucial few; identify what the success factors would be; and then, in varying ways, expose individuals who were holding out and seek a consensus solution. These tasks are obviously easier said than done and often require the patience of Job.

It did not take long for Mauro to get the lay of the land regarding the forces at play. In part, some of this reading of the political winds occurred when Mauro was invited to attend the Premiers' Conference in the summer of 1993. He spoke privately with many of the premiers and could see fairly quickly what broad coalitions of interest existed. In brief, the three NDP governments, of Ontario, Saskatchewan, and B.C., were opposed and/or fearful. Alberta and Manitoba were supportive and aligned with the federal government. The Atlantic provinces were supportive but worried about federal abandonment and regional-development powers. Quebec was favourably disposed but very cautious and, in these early days, raised concerns about communications and culture.

Mauro is credited in many of the provincial camps with playing a constructive and patient role, and with being especially important in three respects. First, he was among the main movers to insist fairly early on that the negotiations needed a text to work from and it could not proceed from just broad conceptual issues. Everyone involved of course understood that having a text was inevitable, but there were differences about how early this ought to occur, and how detailed the text needed to be. As a lawyer, Mauro favoured having a text, but some of the players had different tactical approaches. As a result, to some extent those more familiar with federal–provincial styles of policy making were aligned against those who expected trade-agreement approaches. Trade agreements customarily proceeded with text, including many bracketed (unagreed) items and wordings, that remained, often through meeting after meeting, until the final agreement was reached. This practice was frequently annoying to federal–provincial veterans, who were used to seeing offending passages expunged immediately.

A second area where Mauro's negotiating and facilitating nudges and exhortations were important was in the procurement and dispute-settlement aspects and provisions. Mauro chaired the procurement table. He also saw the dispute-resolution provisions as being crucial to the integrity of the agreement. He had to steer a careful path among the main camps in this regard, but there is little doubt among the practitioners that this was one area where his own expertise and his views nudged him a notch or two above 'neutral.'

A third aspect of Mauro's role was more subtle. In the end-game and in the final phase in June 1994, the meetings themselves became very trying and combative, with tempers on edge. Throughout the entire process, Mauro met with ministers and chief negotiators before and after meetings, and of course conversed by telephone. Thus if an additional final trust factor was needed to get through this final stage, Mauro helped supply some of it. Thus, it is certainly possible to argue that, without his facilitator role, in effect a reasoned 'good cop' presence, the negotiations might have failed.

This is not the same as saying that Mauro was the glue in the process. Other kinds of roles, and kinds of political muscle and skill as well, not to mention a little luck, performed that function. The role of intermediary was also linked to the secretariat. The secretariat was based in Industry Canada in offices nearby the federal negotiating team, and thus faced concerns (its own and the provinces') about maintaining its independence in support of the co-chairs and Art Mauro. The secretariat, moreover, tended to be staffed by persons who were federal–provincial relations–oriented rather than the 'trade' types that comprised the federal negotiating team. The secretariat staff were strong supporters of the need for an agreement, and indeed for several years had 'carried the torch' for internal trade, often in great frustration at the lack of ministerial action. But now that negotiations were under way, they also had to be neutral, or at least independent. They were not always seen this way. Some provinces saw them as federal stalking horses, whereas some members of the federal negotiating team saw them as perhaps too pro-provincial or as insufficiently energetic about supporting the federal agenda.

However, the troops in the secretariat deserve considerable credit for, first, keeping the issue on the internal government agenda in the 'down years' of the later 1980s and, then, for administratively keeping the operation going in the semi-chaotic and tense final stages, when the negotiators depended on having appropriate briefing material, amended text, and supportive mediation at the level of officials.

As for the provincial teams and their secretariats, it is important to note their varying inherent capacities in, and organizational approaches towards, the negotiations. First, as we have seen, there were differences in the degree to which the key negotiators came from federal–provincial relations career experiences as opposed to trade backgrounds. Saskatchewan and Alberta tended towards the former, while Ontario and Quebec had more of the latter. Second, there were differences in the degree to which there was a government-wide commitment to the negotiations. All provincial governments had, in one form or another, to obtain negotiating mandates from Cabinet, but certainly in some instances it was unclear whether negotiators were speaking, or could speak, for 'the government.'

A final feature of provincial capacities was the simple ability to mobilize resources. The smaller provinces were almost inevitably outgunned in this regard by the larger provinces. All provinces also had to make use of expertise and negotiators that only their various line departments possessed. Thus the various sectoral tables were typically manned by line-department experts and were influenced, as chapters 5, 6, and 7 show, by the policy-field cultures and prior agendas that participants brought to bear in these fields.

Conclusions

The core of the internal-trade agreement was a battle over general rules versus exceptions and legitimate objectives. The political fault lines also involved dispute-settlement provisions and the role of regional policy and Crown corporations. Procurement and investment issues also loomed large in the end-game. The final pact was the product of a negotiating and political (including personal) interplay among the federal government, a neutral chair and secretariat, and twelve provincial/territorial governments. As in any complex multi-party negotiation conducted over a twelve-month period, the nature of the interplay had both permanent or stable alliances and shifting ones. We have by no means been able to capture all the subtleties of the process, but some broad patterns are evident from the analysis above.

The federal government, the secretariat, Alberta, and Manitoba were the most supportive of an agreement that maximized the general rules and effective dispute-settlement provisions and minimized the exceptions. They were the most inclined to see the AIT as being a trade agreement. Quebec was also supportive, and indeed the presence of both Alberta and Quebec as allies of the federal government was an interesting reversal of many of the normal recent configurations of federal–provincial politics, wherein they were often the most truculent about federal intentions.

The three provincial NDP governments did not agree with one another on every matter – far from it – but they were united strategically and philosophically by scepticism about a free-trade agenda in general, and about the federal government's intentions. Ontario, B.C., and Saskatchewan led the forces that would have preferred a sectoral approach, but, failing that, in the resulting agreement sought to maximize the exceptions and legitimate objectives and to minimize general rules and dispute settlement.

In some other respects Quebec fell into its own category. It was supportive of an internal-trade agreement, but its negotiating approach was inevitably couched in terms of an expected election. It had to show support for an economic union without giving up or appearing to give up provincial powers. The possibility of a Parti Québécois separatist victory was the unstated bottom line for those provinces which otherwise might be tempted to walk away from the negotiations. Had they done so, federalism would have visibly failed for the third time in four years on a major negotiation, leaving federalist forces in Quebec without any strong evidence of a flexible relationship between Quebec and the rest of Canada.

The remaining players, the Atlantic provinces and the two territorial governments, eventually signed the agreement from a position of recognized political weakness, in a negotiating sense. They saw the internal-trade agreement as a partial opportunity, but some also saw it as an exercise in damage control, where defensive postures were the only real option.

The agreement, however, cannot be fully appreciated only at the general level. There are other features and other dynamics that emerge from the sectoral tables, and it is to an account of several of these that we turn in the next three chapters.

5

Sectoral Negotiations I:
Procurement and Regional Policy

We have already reviewed some of the ways in which government procurement policies and regional policy affected both the historical run-up
to the AIT negotiations and the core negotiating dynamics among the
thirteen governments involved in the negotiation. However, a closer
examination is needed to fully appreciate the free-trade-versus-federalism
and governance tensions and issues. As mentioned in chapter 1, the
grouping or clustering of sectors in this and the next two chapters is
based on a mixture of rationales, including: close linkages and tensions in
the actual negotiations (certainly the case in this chapter); common trade
or policy characteristics (the framework nature of the three sectors, in
chapter 6); and natural resource and related resource ownership characteristics (as in chapter 7).

We look first at procurement, the largest chapter in the agreement
(Chapter 5) and at regional policy (the two-page Article 1801). The two
areas are in fact interwoven and, to a considerable extent, are, two sides
of the same coin. Indeed, the fact that regional-development policy is
only a two-page clause in the AIT is partially misleading since mini-
regional provisions also exist, as we will see in this and later chapters of
the agreement.

As an analytical backdrop to the two parts of this chapter, it is important
to appreciate some of the precursors of the procurement and regional-
policy debate in the evolution of international-trade regimes. Procurement
under GATT was always treated as a fairly major exemption to liberalized
trade principles largely on the grounds that procurement involved purchases by the nation-state on behalf of its taxpayers and that such taxpayers
would want to buy wherever possible from national suppliers. Gradually, in
successive GATT rounds and in the recent FTA and NAFTA, procurement

became subject in part to liberalized trade rules of non-discrimination through the successive lowering of threshold levels and through requirements for greater transparency and open bidding. Amounts above a given threshold would be subject to open bidding from other countries' suppliers, while those below would not. Other kinds of exceptions would also affect procurement, such as in the realm of defence.

It was always argued in these debates that taxpayers have an interest as well in efficient procurement choices both in the sense of being able to purchase goods at the lowest competitive price and in relation to obtaining the best-quality items available at that price. But the domestic history of procurement debates was also influenced by earlier instances of corruption, where politicians, bureaucrats, and firms played patronage politics. Concerns about the honesty and probity of purchases are accordingly central to the procurement process, especially through the transparency and fairness of the bidding system.

Another strand in the procurement debate is that procurement of goods may be different from procurement of services. The former are typically easier to specify, with objective standards, whereas the latter have a greater qualitative judgmental mix. Service provision may also not require the service provider to establish in another jurisdiction.

The connections of this history of procurement to regional policy is both direct and indirect. Regional policy can refer to policies and programs overtly designated as such, where a given spatial region (subnational, subprovincial, city, or rural area) is accorded special incentives by the state in order to reduce economic disparities or inequalities (Savoie 1986; McGee 1992). In this context, procurement may simply be one part of the array of incentives. Regional economic-development policy can also be more general in that nations can simply favour internal spatial areas through an array of policies whose effect is favourable to a given area but the intent of which is not regional *per se.*

In international-trade terms, regional policy became bound up in debates about subsidies. If government spending or other programs or actions favour particular firms or industrial sectors in such a way as to allow them to reduce prices and penetrate foreign markets in an unfair or trade-distorting manner, another country's competitor firms may allege that such practices are illegal subsidies that can be countervailed under trade law (Bence and Smith 1989; OECD 1990). However, programs that favour regions (i.e., spatial/geographic areas) may or may not be subsidies because they may or may not be sector-specific. Gradually, various international-trade arrangements have been able to discipline such regional policies, but only to a limited extent. For example, the WTO negotiations which were proceeding concurrent with the AIT resulted in provisions that gave 'assistance to disadvantaged regions,' a non-actionable status, provided that they met 'neutral and objective criteria' and were carried out pursuant to 'a general framework of regional development.' As we see below, similar 'disciplining' mechanisms became a part of the internal-trade debate in Canada.

Procurement

In many respects the work completed on government procurement in the AIT's Chapter 5 represents the sectoral 'centrepiece' of the agreement. The procurement chapter is arguably the most comprehensive of the AIT as it establishes a framework for procurement practices to ensure equal access in a transparent and efficient manner for Canadian suppliers, regardless of their location in the country. Designed to lower the cost of procurement, which runs in the order of $50 billion annually for both the provincial and federal governments, chapter 5 has the biggest potential economic impact of any of the agreement's chapters. As a result, the procurement chapter was also the most politically important of the AIT in terms of striking the deal overall.

Key Provisions

In keeping with the overarching principles of the AIT, Chapter 5 is designed to 'establish a framework that will ensure equal access to procurement for all Canadian suppliers in order to contribute to a reduction in purchasing costs and the development of a strong economy in a context of transparency and efficiency' (Canada 1994, 17). Also in keeping with the precedent established by other sectoral tables, the chapter on procurement does not limit itself to the general rules of the agreement (Part III, Chapter 4). In particular, Chapter 5 applies its own rules of reciprocal non-discrimination and transparency 'customized' for the specific sectoral concerns of government procurement.

Article 502 sets the parameters for the scope and coverage of procurement. As the 'chapeau clause,' Article 502.1 establishes that the chapter applies to the practices of all party entities contained in Annex 502.1A, where the procurement value is:

(a) $25,000 or greater, in cases where the largest portion of the procurement is for goods;

(b) $100,000 or greater, in cases where the largest portion of the procurement is for services, except those services excluded by Annex 502.1B; or

(c) $100,000 or greater, in the case of construction.

Annex 502.1A presents an impressive list that includes all government departments 'proper' and a wide-ranging number of agencies, boards, corporations, and commissions that are involved in procurement within Canada, even if the good or service is intended for use outside Canada, such as the purchases made by the federal Canadian International Development Agency (CIDA).

There are, however, major areas of exclusion. Annex 502.1B excludes services provided by licensed professionals, including doctors, engineers, architects, accountants, and lawyers; locally owned trucks used for hauling on highway construction; services provided for organizing sporting events; services relating to the analysis and/or management of financial investments, including those of governments; health and social services; and advertising and public-relation services. Also excluded from coverage under the chapter are entities that are not accountable to executive branches of government, entities whose objective is national security, entities that are of a commercial nature and/or are in direct competition with private-sector entities, and entities that are classified as state monopolies. Most visible on this list are the provincial entities that deal with hydro-electric energy and entities in the financial sector, including the Bank of Canada. Also excluded are entities of the so-called MASH sector (municipalities, academic institutions, and social-service and health entities), although Article 502.4 ties the parties to working towards an extended agreement including the MASH sector by 30 June 1996. Work on this is still under way.

In addition to the exceptions allowed for in Article 502, Article 507 outlines the rules for non-application. Specifically, Chapter 5 does not apply to:

(a) procurement of goods intended for resale to the public;

(b) procurement of goods, services or construction purchased on behalf of an entity not covered by this chapter;

(c) procurement from philanthropic institutions, prison labour or persons with disabilities;

(d) procurement contracts between entities listed in the Annexes to Article 502;

(e) procurement of goods, services or construction purchased for representational purposes outside the territory of a Party; and

(f) procurement of any goods the interprovincial movement of which is restricted by laws not inconsistent with this agreement.

Reciprocal non-discrimination is the central philosophy of the agreement on Internal Trade. As indicated above, the procurement chapter follows the spirit of this theme and enhances it with a list of examples of discriminatory practices in the procurement sector. Article 504 provides that, subject to the provisions regarding legitimate objectives (Article 404), each party, including the federal government, shall accord to the goods and services of another party, or to the suppliers of goods and services of another party, no less favourable treatment than it accords its own such goods and services or its own suppliers of such goods and services. Exceptions to this rule can be made on the basis of a preference for Canadian value-added or to the limiting of tendering to Canadian suppliers of goods and services, subject to compliance with any international obligations. In essence though, Article 504 restricts a party's ability to discriminate on the basis of out-of-party criteria. Examples of discriminatory behaviour include, but are not restricted to (Article 504.3), the biasing of technical specifications, residency restrictions, unfair timing in offers for tender, or the use of price discounts or preferential margins to favour given suppliers.

In terms of the valuation of procurement, Article 505 requires a party to disclose, at the time of a call for tender, the full value of the procurement contract. In addition, Article 505.3 states that no entity 'shall prepare, design or otherwise structure a procurement, select a valuation method or divide procurement requirements in order to avoid the obligations of this chapter.' This provision works to prohibit 'contract-splitting' as a means to avoid qualifying for treatment under Article 502. Article 506 outlines the rules for procurement procedures, including tendering practices.

As we discuss further below, Article 508, on regional and economic development, is perhaps the most contentious article in the procurement chapter as it establishes the rules jurisdictions must follow with respect to their use of procurement barriers as policy instruments for regional economic development. Any exclusion of a procurement from under the umbrella of the procurement chapter must be done in such a way as to not impair unduly the access of another party. The excluding party must seek to minimize discriminatory effects and ensure that the exclusion is not more trade restrictive than necessary to achieve its legitimate objective. In addition, the parties could include a list of 'transitional' and 'nonconforming' procurement measures under Article 508.3 and 508.4. Article 508.3 enabled Ontario and Quebec to phase out the exclusion of each other's information technology procurement by 1 January 1996. Of crucial importance, Article 508.4 maintained the national industrial and regional benefits policy, allowing the federal government to pursue national industrial and regional benefits in procurement decisions exceeding $2 million.

Dispute-resolution procedures are quite particular for the procurement chapter. It establishes different bid-protest procedures for the provinces and the federal government. (Government-to-government protests are covered by Chapter 17 of the agreement.) Article 513 refers to the provinces; Article 514, to the federal government. For the provinces, a supplier who makes a complaint does so in the context of the overall dispute-resolution procedures of the AIT – namely, Article 1712 (Initiation of Proceedings by Persons). Under such a circumstance a central review panel is struck, with the aid of the Internal Trade Secretariat. This panel adjudicates and reports on the complaint. Article 514, on the other hand, does not refer to chapter 17. Instead, it stipulates that complainants will appeal directly to an independent third party, or reviewing authority. As is discussed in more detail below, the institution of two separate resolution procedures reflected the different interests of the provinces and the federal government.

Finally, Article 517 established time-lines for future negotiations on the extension of the procurement. The inclusion of the MASH sector and the further achievement of reciprocity of Crown corporations from Annex 502.2A were deemed particularly important.

Negotiating Dynamics

Historically, government procurement in Canada was seen to be under the control of individual jurisdictions. However, with the publication in the mid-1980s of the Macdonald Commission report and the recommendations contained in the intergovernmental paper on regional economic development referred to in chapter 3, procurement seen in the context of 'free trade' between jurisdictions began to receive some attention. Indeed, barriers to procurement were acknowledged to be the most significant in economic terms and received early attention from First Ministers as political awareness grew around the issues of interprovincial barriers writ large.

At the time that the Committee of Ministers of Internal Trade (CMIT) was formed, in November 1987, procurement was one of the three initial 'sectoral challenges' that were to be addressed. Several regional procurement agreements emerged in response to this new political impetus, including the Western Trade Barriers Reduction Agreement (1989) and the Atlantic Government Procurement Agreement (1989, expanded in 1991). In addition, late 1991 saw CMIT present a first-draft outline of what would eventually end up as chapter 5 of the AIT when it outlined the principles of the Intergovernmental Agreement on Goods Procurement. In late 1993 and early 1994, two bilateral agreements on the 'opening of public procurement' were struck between Quebec and New Brunswick and Quebec and Ontario, respectively. However, it was not until December 1993, when sectoral negotiations began in earnest, that a comprehensive multilateral approach to the reduction of procurement barriers was established.

From the outset, the overall objective of these multilateral negotiations was to establish an open and efficient system that provided fair and equitable access to public-sector procurement, regardless of jurisdictional location in Canada. In practical terms, such a system would eliminate discriminatory procurement policies (e.g., tendering) that acted on the basis of jurisdictional boundaries, and would create a level playing field for all Canadian suppliers to bid on procurement contracts. As with other sectors (and the AIT as a whole), the new procurement system would have to be based on the fundamentals of reciprocal non-discrimination and transparency.

Not surprisingly, the procurement table achieved quick and unanimous support of the broad principles of reciprocal non-discrimination and transparency, not only because these were the central principles of the AIT, but also because several of the jurisdictions had recent experience with tearing down procurement barriers at the bilateral or regional provincial levels, or, in the case of the federal government, at the international level with the FTA, NAFTA, and GATT. It was widely accepted that non-discrimination and transparency were vital to establish the proper (i.e., efficient) balance between Canadian suppliers and their governments. In addition, negotiations on the acceptable level of thresholds in the 'chapeau clause' (Article 502) were relatively non-acrimonious. Again, this was due to experience with levels set in, for example, the Ontario/Quebec agreement. And although the federal negotiators pushed initially for lower threshold levels in an effort to be consistent with NAFTA and GATT, the limits established in the AIT were arrived at easily and quickly.

Far more difficult, however, was the identification of those entities to be included under the auspices of the thresholds, and the qualifications of discriminating behaviour. In one respect the debate here centred on the definition or language of what was deemed to be a 'Canadian good' or what constituted 'Canadian value-added.' Two provinces in particular, British Columbia and Alberta, pushed for a definition based on what is 'sold in Canada,' whereas Ontario and Quebec supported a more 'international' definition of Canadian content or value. In the end, the clause is rather more permissive than it is mandatory, and allows for a case-by-case investigation of content at the procuring jurisdictions' discretion. In essence, the clause establishes the outer limits or most restrictive formulation, permitting less restrictive practices by any participating government.

The other aspect of difficult debate revolved around listing examples of discriminatory behaviour. In large part this exercise was aimed at 'customizing' the meaning of non-discrimination in chapter 5. In a more tangible way, though, it also had to do with the interpretation of what 'reciprocal' meant with respect to Crown corporations.

Federal and provincial Crown corporations had been established across the decades for a variety of reasons, but these usually included some form of social or regional-provincial development rationale (Hardin 1974; Tupper and Doern 1981, 1988; Laux and Molot 1988). The argument about Crown corporations was divided into two issues – namely, the use of such entities for industrial or regional economic development, and the use of them as quasi-private, independent entities. Agencies used for regional-development purposes were either covered in Article 508 or excluded from the chapter altogether due to the difficulties in reaching agreement (for example, on entities such as the Canadian Space Agency).

Quasi-private Crown corporations were covered in the non-intervention 'doctrine,' which confirmed that governments were not to intervene in the procurement practices of such organizations. A key concern here was the huge provincial electric utilities. And although it is somewhat difficult to monitor such intervention, it was acknowledged that any regulations for procurement in this sector could impose costs or constraints that would go against the rationale of quasi-private corporations in the first place. Still, Ontario was concerned with what 'reciprocal' meant in this context, attempting to establish the 'right' to 'reciprocate' in its territory the treatment accorded it by a party in another territory. In the final analysis, though, Ontario offered to cover all of its Crown corporations under the condition that chapter 5 guarantee that all outstanding agencies would be dealt with in the following year.

Finally, with respect to thresholds and non-discrimination, the decision not to include the MASH sector under Article 502 was reached easily, even though all parties acknowledged that it was an important sector. Essentially, it was the complexity of the issues in the sector, coupled with the time constraints for negotiations, that resulted in the exemption of the MASH sector but with the promise for future negotiations in one year. In addition, it was understood that MASH-sector negotiations would be easier to complete once a standardized reporting and electronic tendering system was put in place, as in the requirements of Article 511.

With reference specifically to the issues of information and reporting contained in Article 511, agreement in principle about the necessity for a common electronic tendering system to lower the costs of transacting business was easily reached. As one might expect, however, some disagreement was evident when it came time to choose 'which,' or, more to the point 'whose,' tendering system was to be chosen.

The most contentious issue at the procurement sectoral table had to do with regional and economic development (Article 508) and the ability of jurisdictions to use procurement as a policy instrument in this regard. As was commonplace in other sectors, the debate here revolved around the battle between provinces that wanted a broad list of exceptions and those that wanted a very limited range of exceptions. Essentially, these 'camps' in the procurement chapter were no different from those in other chapters, with Saskatchewan, British Columbia, and the Atlantic provinces pushing for wide exemptions, while Alberta, Manitoba, and, to a lesser degree, Ontario and Quebec pushed for limited exemptions. Also common to many of the other chapters was the fact that final resolution of these matters did not result until the last meetings at the ministerial level. The article reflects a 'one-off' approach to exceptions that differs from the general regional and economic-development objectives (Article 101.4[c]) which were deemed to be too broad and would have resulted in the complete 'gutting' of the chapter.

Less typical of other sectoral chapters was the role played by the federal government with respect to regional and economic-development exceptions in procurement. Whereas the federal teams were usually seen as staunch supporters of very limited exceptions, in the procurement sector a strong push was made for exempting the Industrial and Regional Benefits Program (IRBP). In fact, the relationship between the Internal Trade Secretariat and other federal entities, such as Western Economic Diversification Canada and the Atlantic Canada Opportunities Agency, on this matter was contentious. The ITS was pushing for a threshold level in the order of $20 million. In the final analysis, the ITS received a concession of 10 per cent of that figure, resulting in the $2-million threshold covered in Article 508. Indeed, the exclusion of the federal IRBP is a significant example of a federal exception in the AIT as a whole.

Running a close second in terms of contention to the regional-development exceptions were the issues of bid-protest procedures in the dispute-resolution mechanism. Here, the debate revolved around the choice (or not) of a common procedure for both federal and provincial jurisdictions. The federal government was strongly in favour of instituting a procedure closely matched to that covered under NAFTA – namely, a system that allows for independent third-party analysis of disputes (e.g., the use of the Canadian International Trade Tribunal). The federal model argued in favour of allowing for supplier complaints without the necessity of government-to-government discussions. The provinces, on the other hand, argued that such a mechanism had the appearance of a quasi-judicial process and was unnecessary for the resolution of disputes among jurisdictions that were all 'friends.' As a result of this disagreement, the procurement chapter establishes the previously mentioned different bid-protest mechanisms for each jurisdictional level: the federal model (Article 5.14) is very NAFTA-like; the provincial model (Article 5.13) closely matches the mechanism outlined in chapter 17 of the AIT.

Procurement in the Broader AIT Context

As we have indicated elsewhere, the negotiation of the AIT brought together two policy communities that had relatively little experience with each other – the trade community and the federal–provincial community. Perhaps nowhere were the dynamics resulting from this meeting of communities more evident than in the bargaining over Chapter 5. In particular, the federally led initiative for a very 'trade-like' chapter closely resembling recent experiences with NAFTA and GATT was met with resistance from the provincial communities who saw procurement much more as policy instruments for regional and economic development than as trade policy. For instance, the federal push for lower threshold values resembling GATT and NAFTA and a third party–led resolution mechanism met with provincial resistance. The fact that different bid-protest mechanisms are contained in the chapter is proof of the difficulty negotiators had in gaining consistency for jurisdictional level, perhaps indicating a federal 'win' on bid protest, whereas the higher threshold levels agreed to represent a provincial 'win.' Ironically, however, the resolution of the regional and economic-development exceptions seems to favour the federal side more than the provincial, given the important exception of the federal IRBP.

The list of exceptions leads one to consider the impact that chapter 5 has on the broader relationship between jurisdictions in terms of their policy 'power.' One view of this relationship is to see the AIT as a potential extension of the federal trade-and-commerce power, coupled with the disciplining of provincial powers. In particular, the exception of the federal IRBP, seemingly at the expense of the provincial regional and economic-development powers of procurement policy, appears to support this conclusion. The extent to which this conclusion can be broadly drawn will also play itself out in the ongoing negotiations surrounding the so-called MASH sector.

As was indicated earlier, the MASH sector was left out of Chapter 5, owing to its complex and contentious nature. In part, the issue was the fact that the MASH sector is under provincial jurisdictional control, and yet the federal government wanted a role in the negotiations. If anything, this role is to be that of 'overseerer.' Still, the federal negotiators clearly have a stake in reducing the capacity of provinces to use procurement in the MASH sector as a discriminatory policy tool, because of both the federal philosophy of 'free trade' and the principles of regional individual equality of access. Interestingly, though, the recent changes to federally funded programs in the MASH sector, as contained in the new Canada Health and Social Transfer (CHST), arguably *increase* provincial discretionary power for social-program implementation – seemingly running counter to the internal-trade philosophy. However, if the federal team can ensure the reduction of as many barriers as possible in this sector – read: the reduction of policy flexibility – then perhaps changes in CHST can be offset by the provisions of Chapter 5. The results of these developments remain to be seen.

Regional Economic Policies: The Presence at Every Table

The regional-economic-development provisions of the AIT were primarily negotiated at the main table of chief negotiators, but there were also regional dimensions in several chapters of the AIT. We have already seen this in the procurement area, discussed above. However, it is Article 1801 that contains the central provisions regarding regional economic development.

Key Provisions

The first paragraph of Article 1801 supplies a broad statement of the types of objectives that measures geared towards regional economic development can be used to achieve. Thus the parties agree that a general framework of regional economic development can play an important roles 'in encouraging long-term job creation, economic growth or industrial competitiveness or in reducing regional disparities.'

Article 1801.2 then provides an exception for measures which are a part of a general framework of regional economic development. An exception applies provided that it does not have the effect of unduly impairing the 'access of persons, goods, services or investments' of other parties. Moreover, the exception cannot be more trade-restrictive than necessary to achieve the regional-economic-development objective.

The three clauses of Article 1801 deal with transparency provisions which are the main line of defence of mechanisms for 'disciplining' the regional exception. There are provisions that each party must notify all other parties of its existing programs relating to regional economic development, and of new ones, 'on adoption' (1801.3c). Annual reports on such programs are also to be prepared. Evaluations are to be conducted and published every five years.

For greater clarity, paragraph 6 of Article 1801 indicates that the exceptions clause does not apply to two annexes which list obligations from other chapters. One lists obligations which the parties have made to eliminate, phase out, or liberalize in five other chapters. Another lists whole chapters to which Article 1801.2 does not apply.

Crucial to the regional debate is the question of what constitutes a 'general framework of regional development.' Article 1801.8 indicates that it must be a program or statute-based system identified by the party as promoting regional economic development. It must also contain specific eligibility criteria and be generally available to those that meet such criteria. Moreover, reasonable performance or economic-development objectives must be specified that are capable of being measured.

However, this definition is clouded considerably by provisions in 1801.9 inserted at the insistence of Quebec. These specify that a general framework may also include 'a decentralized, cooperative approach by way of a system of delegated authority to provincial regions or sub-regions.' But these in turn must be contained in framework agreements, with priorities and periods specified.

Negotiating Dynamics

Focused discussions on an overall regional development article did not really begin until late February 1994, when the chief negotiators took up what they knew would be a difficult issue. As text was initially examined, Nova Scotia first wanted a paragraph added to the non-discrimination general principles stating that the non-discrimination provision would not affect the ability of the federal government to discriminate for the purposes of regional economic development.

Another slant on the regional text came from Newfoundland. It suggested that there be special provisions for 'lesser developed provinces' and that such provinces not be expected to make contributions in the name of reciprocity that were inconsistent with their individual development. Developed provinces would recognize this state of affairs explicitly. Newfoundland chose the terminology 'lesser developed provinces' to parallel that in international-trade agreements, which always had special provisions for lesser developed countries. Canada's easternmost province had heard from the outset of the negotiations how federal and other parties wanted concepts related to international-trade agreements to apply. However, Newfoundland argued that, if this was so, one had to take all of the logic of such international agreements rather than just what suited some parties. Hence, special provisions for 'lesser developed' provinces were advocated.

The federal government and Alberta strongly opposed the use of this kind of terminology but did recognize that regional issues had to be addressed. Ontario's preference was for regional-development issues to be addressed in each sectoral chapter.

From a very early stage, the chief negotiators agreed that there was an important distinction to be made between regional and economic development. But exactly how this distinction would be made remained contentious. So also was the issue of symmetry between the regional-economic-development programs of the federal and provincial governments. When it seemed consensus could not be reached on these issues, chief negotiators established a working group to try to hammer out an agreement.

The working group reported in early May 1994 to both chief negotiators, and shortly thereafter to internal-trade ministers. The politicians wanted regional issues to be handled in each sectoral chapter, but some provinces, such as Newfoundland, Nova Scotia, and Saskatchewan, would not give up the right to have a general article on regional economic development. This was in part because no one could be sure what in fact was being agreed to in the sectoral chapters by the other sectoral tables.

As discussions and negotiations proceeded, Quebec raised concerns about the requirements for consultations prior to developing regional programs. It argued that such a provision would slow down its ability to respond to its regional-development needs. This requirement was eliminated, but new requirements for a written annual report were added. Quebec also succeeded in getting the above-mentioned Article 1801.9, which included the provision that framework policies for regional economic development could include a decentralized, cooperative approach by way of a system of delegated authority to provincial regions and subregions. This levered open considerably the range of things that might be considered regional framework policies.

If several provinces were moving to open up space for regional policy, there were also counter-pressures from others to prevent slippage. For example, the federal government, Alberta, Manitoba, and Ontario sought to ensure that certain disciplines in sector chapters, such as those on open bidding for government procurement, could not be overridden by the general exception made for regional economic development. These were handled by the items listed in Annex 1802.6, as mentioned above.

Conclusions

The fact that procurement and overall regional-economic-development aspects of the AIT were handled by the chief negotiators and had major ministerial involvement testifies to the central place these issues occupied politically and economically. It is fair to say that the AIT opens up more procurement to pan-Canadian bidding. But is also true that a lot of the legwork for this liberalization had been done by the previously signed regional procurement agreements.

It is also reasonable to conclude that the general use of policies governing regional economic development has been disciplined to a greater extent than before. The disciplining comes in part from events outside the AIT – namely, the reduction of fiscal capacity by most governments. But it also comes from the AIT provisions for defining framework policies for regional development and providing transparent criteria and some reporting requirements.

At the same time, the larger importance of regional economic development and the vagueness as to how to assess general economic-development policies, as distinct from explicit regional policies, remain. These issues and dynamics are still ingrained in the very nature of governing in a federation and in a pan-continental Canada, where economic regions are simply too diverse for only trade-driven rules to prevail. These issues had to be and were fudged in the AIT, just as they had been in the procurement/national/regional bargains struck in international-trade agreements.

6

Sectoral Negotiations II: Investment, Labour Mobility, and Environment

We now look at a second cluster of sectoral negotiations that took place in three tables or arenas: investment, labour mobility, and environment. Each policy field may well be only a chapter in the AIT, but each is complex and has its own considerable policy history. Hence, in each of the three sections below, the purpose of the analysis is to supply only a basic overview of the issues, negotiating and decision-making dynamics, and main outcomes for each sector.

It is also important to recall from chapter 1 that the 'sector' chapters and tables were in fact not typically sectors, in the sense of vertical industrial sectors such as steel or autos. Indeed, the three sectors explored here are aspects of internal trade that are horizontal, and hence they cut across all or most sectors of the economy. The account in chapter 7 of three resource sectors comes closer to dealing with vertical sectors of the economy, although even this is debatable.

These sectoral negotiations should also be seen in four important contexts. First, they were typically negotiated by officials and experts from the other relevant line departments of the governments involved. Second, many of the issues and policy problems they were dealing with had been in their sector's agenda for years. Accordingly, one of the issues is whether the internal-trade arena of decision making simply continued the process without much change or whether it altered the dynamics precisely because it was a different political-economic arena for such decisions. Third, each sectoral table was given different degrees of independence from the main table. All tables had to have their agreements integrated in some way with the main table, particularly regarding whether general rules or sectoral or chapter rules would take precedence. Fourth, the sectoral tables had the potential to involve sectoral or issue-based interest groups. The book in general does not focus on the interest-group politics of the agreement. This is the case, in part because the strategy in most jurisdictions, as previous chapters have shown, was not to involve interest groups in any fully consultative way. Nonetheless, in the accounts below, glimpses of interest-group realities and politics are presented.

Investment

Key Provisions

The investment provisions in Chapter 6 of the agreement were, in many respects, the centrepiece of the negotiations regarding the mobility of capital in the Canadian economic union. Article 603 specifies the parties' agreement with the principle of reciprocal non-discrimination, whereby each party agrees that it will accord treatment to an investor of a party 'no less favourable than the best treatment it accords, in like circumstances,' to an investor of any party. Article 604 contains an agreement that in essence prohibits parties from setting local presence and residency requirements as a condition, for the establishment or acquisition of an enterprise.

Article 607 deals with the issue of performance requirements. With respect to goods and services, it is clear that no party can impose or enforce, or condition, the receipt of an incentive on compliance with any requirement to: achieve a specific level or percentage of local content of goods or services; purchase or use goods and services produced locally; or purchase goods or services from a local source. Such conditions can be applied, as Article 607 further sets out, when the goal of creating or maintaining employment is involved and for the purposes of regional economic development, provided that certain related principles are followed.

Annex 608.3 to the investment chapter contains an agreed-upon 'Code of Conduct on Incentives' that was crucial to the agreement as a whole. Under it the parties affirm the application of operating principles regarding incentives they may offer, and commit to minimizing the adverse effects of their incentives on the economic interests of other parties. Certain kinds of incentives are prohibited under the code. These include an incentive that is contingent on, and would directly result in, an enterprise located in one province or territory relocating an existing operation to another. Incentives that would allow the recipient enterprise to undercut competitors in another Canadian jurisdiction in obtaining a contract are also prohibited.

The parties also agree to avoid certain incentives. Regional-development incentives are allowed, but the parties agree that they will endeavour to refrain from incentives that: sustain for an extended period of time an economically non-viable operation whose production adversely affects the competitive position of a facility located in the territory of another party; increases capacity in sectors where the increase is not warranted by market conditions; or is excessive, either in absolute terms or relative to the total value of the specific project.

The investment chapter and the code on incentives provide for several reporting mechanisms, including annual reports on incentives, as well as requirements to notify parties of the details of any measure.

Within the chapter there are also provisions which limit the application of the freedom of movement of capital. First, where there are inconsistencies between the investment chapter and other chapters in Part IV of the agreement, the other chapter prevails to the extent of the inconsistency. Second, many areas of government procurement by a set of listed agencies are exempt from the internal-trade agreement as a whole. Third, legitimate objectives can be used to justify a measure that otherwise might be contrary to the principles in the chapter. These include regional-development measures, as we have already examined in chapter 5 of this book.

Not surprisingly, these investment provisions reflected a compromise between unbridled notions of the mobility of capital and a more constrained version (OECD 1991; Investment Canada 1991). The tensions between these two are well known, but the background context for them within Canada is dual in nature. In part they are a product of the longer-term legacy of policies governing regional economic development, examined in chapters 2 and 5. But they are also the product of the debates and policies within Canada on foreign ownership and investment (Safarian 1993; Smythe 1996).

From the mid to late 1960s until the early 1980s, this policy area focused on federal policies that leaned broadly to the screening of foreign investment, including provisions for performance requirements. The focal point for this activity was the former Foreign Investment Review Agency (FIRA), but it had other manifestations in areas such energy policy as well (Doern and Toner 1985). These federal and central Canada (especially Ontario)-inspired policies were also contentious in some provinces which simply wanted any kind of inward investment to help provincial and local development. From 1984 on, particularly with the transformation of FIRA into Investment Canada, federal policy focused much more on encouraging investment (Smythe 1996). Screening criteria and thresholds for review were altered so as to exhibit to the world a welcoming attitude to investment.

These policy trends continued in the successive FTA, NAFTA, and GATT rounds of trade negotiations, where investment provisions became ever more central, though always constrained by some exceptions which Canada and other nation-states insisted upon (Trebilcock and Howse 1995). In these international negotiating realms, the equivalent to 'legitimate objectives' came under a variety of topics, including cultural industries, banking, national security, and the like.

Negotiating Dynamics and Issues

Because the investment chapter was very much federally led, it is also important to note that the international-trade negotiations provided a major impetus in three respects. First, the values of freedom of capital movement were in the ascendency. Second, the experts in the government who headed the Canadian articulation of this view were centred in Investment Canada, which, as of the summer of 1993, was now fully a part of Industry Canada. Industry Canada's ADM for policy was from Investment Canada, and hence there was an extra degree of interest in this area in the larger Industry Canada set of priorities (Doern 1996). Third, the international-trade agreements had required considerable textual language, and hence certain kinds of concepts and provisions were second nature to the federal regulators and to a small subset of the provincial ones as well (Ontario and Quebec in particular). The federal negotiators from Industry Canada were thus well motivated and disposed to see the extension of these investment framework rules into the domestic market. Indeed, the case could readily be made that what had already been agreed to by Canada in these agreements simply required the provinces to follow suit.

As was to be the case in several areas of the AIT, there were different basic philosophical postures adopted. Most of the provinces favoured a case-by-case approach in which one listed investment barriers and then worked out how to reduce or get rid of them. The federal government favoured a principles-based approach derived from the international-trade context and realities. However, this garnered suspicion in many provincial camps that the investment provisions were a key part of the federal government's alleged hidden agenda. The 'feds,' it was thought by some, would use the investment provisions to get done what they could not get done in NAFTA and other negotiations.

Some of the tensions in the negotiations were aided by the fact that the federal government chaired the investment negotiating table. In other words, the head of the federal investment negotiating team was also the chair of the table. As the head of the federal negotiating team, she had a strong agenda and was pushing it on behalf of the federal government against many reluctant and opposing provinces. But as chair of the table, she was expected by many provincial participants to be neutral. This was clearly a difficult position to be in. Indeed, in the early phases of the negotiation, the federal team did adopt the view that it had to, in certain respects, educate some of their provincial counterparts who were simply less aware of, and less experienced in, the recently evolving world of international-investment regimes and rules.

There were also difficulties in the relations between the investment table and the table of chief negotiators, largely because it was not until quite late in the negotiating process that the other key issues were settled. Inevitably these other issues were precisely those we analysed in chapters 4 and 5: legitimate objectives; procurement, and exceptions therein; and regional-development exemptions. Hence the line-up of provinces on the investment issue were basically similar to those traced in chapter 4, on the macro negotiating politics.

One of the early issues at the investment table was simply how various players viewed the definition and scope of what investment was (Benedickson, Doern, and Olewiler 1994). The federal view was that investment dealt with anything that facilitated doing business. It went beyond the physical establishment of a firm or plant, or even, in the era of globalization, the movement of money. It had to cover firms, individuals, and citizens in their efforts to do business in Canada. For example, as late as April 1994, the federal government's investment negotiator was pointing out to the chief negotiators that the definition of investment was too limiting. At that stage it was defined as 'an enterprise.'

This narrow view was seen as a failure to appreciate the role of capital in investment decision making. The purpose of the investment table was to remove government measures that distort the investment decisions of investors who are primarily concerned about their rate of return. Capital is the vehicle for both making the investment and taking the profit, and thus is intricately involved with the operational activities of firms, including the sale and purchase of goods and services. At the time, some players at the table were linking the definitions of investment with financial institutions, which were excluded from the investment chapter from the beginning. The federal investment negotiators believed that there was confusion in evidence between the use of capital and the source of capital. In the end a broader definition of investment was included in the agreement.

For similar reasons, the federal investment negotiators, and the investment table as a whole, were continuously wary of what might be simultaneously being agreed to in other chapters, including procurement, resource processing, and labour mobility. In short, it was a sectoral chapter group that wanted to be, and saw itself as, a horizontal or framework chapter.

For the provinces there were also negotiating tensions that arose out of the rushed nature under which they had to identify, and eventually list in annexes, which of their measures/agencies would be exempt from the investment provisions. In some cases this was similarly being completed for the just-finishing NAFTA and GATT negotiations as well – hence the suspicion of hidden federal agendas. A few provinces sought to play an old federal–provincial policy game which simply said that if the 'feds' wanted something from them (e.g., a broader investment chapter), they would have to compensate the provinces for it with cash outlays or concessions in other parts of the AIT. For a deficit-reducing government engaged in a major program-review exercise in 1993–4, the game of buying concessions was outmoded and no longer viable (Swimmer 1996).

The investment issues were also clearly linked to the kinds of dispute-resolution provisions. The investment table had to negotiate, however, without really knowing what was happening on that front. The more that the agreement had strong private-access provisions for business, the better the investment chapter provisions would be. If the latter were weak, the investment chapter loses a considerable part of its impact.

As for individual provinces, we have already seen some of their preferred areas of emphasis in our account in chapter 4. Ontario was particularly insistent on the principle of reciprocal non-discrimination because it saw most investment-enticing incentives and policies as being in effect an economic loss for Ontario. British Columbia placed special emphasis on the achievement of the code on investment incentives. Quebec was in one sense broadly supportive of the investment provisions, but it also has the longest list of exempt agencies under the procurement areas of the agreement. Alberta and Manitoba supported the broad thrust of the federal positions but also sought disciplined limitations and new reporting requirements to restrain and make transparent those remaining measures that transgressed the framework rules.

In the end the federal team, as the demandeur, was satisfied that it had extended the frontiers of investment framework rules and thinking, and had broadened its scope. It is several steps removed from a complete liberalization of capital in Canada largely because, in the negotiating dynamics, other views, values, and sources of political and bureaucratic power also held sway.

Labour Mobility

Key Provisions

Chapter 7 of the agreement deals with the mobility of labour. The agreement's purpose is to enable 'any worker qualified for an occupation ... to be granted access to employment opportunities in that occupation' (Article 701). It applies to measures relating to occupational standards, licensing, certification, registration, and residency requirements. But the chapter equally does not apply to various social-policy measures such as labour standards and codes; minimum wages; unemployment-insurance qualification periods; and social-assistance benefits. Article 700 specifies, however, that several of the general rules of the Agreement on Internal Trade do *not* apply to the chapter on labour mobility. Thus, for reasons discussed below, it is fair to say that this chapter is an advance in some respects from the pre–June 1994 situation, but that it is far from being itself a horizontal rules-based regime for one of the four freedoms of a common market.

Negotiating Dynamics and Issues: Uncharted Waters

Unlike the investment and environment chapters, where there had been recent international-trade negotiations to build from and extend, the labour-mobility issues had never really been the subject of a negotiation. In the FTA, NAFTA, and GATT context, this was largely because one was dealing with trade in goods and services and not with the free movement of people. Moreover, in the domestic Canadian context an *overall* negotiation on labour mobility as a whole had never been attempted in a trade-policy sense. Labour mobility had been a part of previous constitutional negotiations. Indeed, the mobility rights of section 6 of the Canadian Charter of Rights and Freedoms was all that remained of proposals that had originally been made by the Trudeau government to entrench the 'economic union' in the constitution. The Mulroney government had tried again in the early 1990s pre-Charlottetown discussions but was rebuffed by the provinces. There had also certainly been disputes in the labour trades and controversies in professional occupations; but, for the negotiators involved, an internal-trade negotiation on the entire subject and in a detailed sense was a totally new experience.

In June 1993, the Council of Ministers of Internal Trade (CMIT) asked the Forum of Labour Market Ministers (FLMM) to handle the negotiations. The FLMM in turn established a working group to develop discussion papers and to send out a questionnaire to ask participants to identify barriers to labour mobility. This initially involved only four provinces: Alberta, Ontario, Quebec, and Nova Scotia. Federal officials were included shortly thereafter.

The provincial representatives came from departments dealing with education or training, and hence they had virtually no experience in trade-like negotiations. Even their federal–provincial experience was far more likely to be in matters such as the negotiation of training grants and programs rather than in regulatory matters. When coupled in these early stages with an absence of clear guidelines from the main table about the negotiations as a whole, it is not surprising that the labour-mobility group got off to a very slow start.

Prior to the main period of negotiations in early 1994, a process of cross-notifications about barriers occurred. The federal government's chief negotiator came from Human Resources and Development Canada (HRCD), and HRDC officials had assembled a long list of specific barriers. This listing process and other early discussions generated a broader examination of the nature and the types of barriers.

The labour mobility table was co-chaired by B.C. and the federal government, but its early membership suffered from a considerable turnover of representatives. Eventually three working groups were established late in 1993, on the definition of barriers, on an external consultation process, and on a review of international and other agreements.

It became clear immediately that the federal government was the main advocate of ensuring that the chapter was as broad in scope as possible. In particular, federal negotiators wanted the chapter to go beyond the traditional boundaries of the provincial ministries involved, which were typically confined to the apprenticeable trades and unskilled employment and training. All barriers for all categories of labour would be involved, in the federal view. The aggressiveness of the federal position was aided by the fact that the negotiating team had a lot of independence or free rein from the main table.

The lead role of the federal government was supported by Alberta and complemented by Manitoba and Quebec. Quebec made considerable substantive input largely through an insistence that the labour-mobility provisions be similar to those relevant sections from GATT and from the treaties that made up the European Union. The main challenge to this view came from Ontario, B.C., and Saskatchewan, as well as Newfoundland. For a province like B.C., concerns were conditioned by its situation, as a receiver of inward migration, whereas for Saskatchewan and Newfoundland problems centred on the outward migration of people.

This latter resistance came largely in the form of arguments which questioned why a rules-based approach was needed, since this was the one chapter that dealt with 'real people.' Rules were not really rules in this case, it was argued, but rather were working principles or guidelines. But the opposition to the agreement from these key provinces was in part a principled opposition but also in part a very pragmatic one.

On the principled side, there were concerns whether provinces could give employment preference to their own citizens in job-creation policies, especially where there was large-scale unemployment and a need to facilitate adjustment. On the pragmatic side, there was the belief in some provinces that the problem of barriers to mobility simply was not all that great. More importantly, there was the practical issue of when and how to deal with a very dense array of self-regulating professional occupations where authority had been legally delegated to such bodies. Not only were these groups influential, but there were, quite simply, a lot of them that would have to be sorted out, often as many as forty professions in each province.

In the negotiation process, three basic kinds of barriers were identified: residency requirements; licensing practices; and the recognition of qualifications. The residency issue was quickly agreed to. Article 706 specifies that no party shall require a worker to be resident in its territory as a condition of: access to employment opportunities; licensing, certification or registration relating to the worker's occupation; or eligibility for the worker's occupation.

The issue of qualification was quite divisive. The federal government's initial position was that of promoting harmonized national standards. This emerged from its earlier work, including papers from the Canadian Labour Force Development Board, which had strongly recommended that national standards were the way to go. This had been suggested even for areas such as tourism, where the labour qualifications were more voluntary in nature. The federal chief negotiator for the chapter pressed hard for standards based on objective competencies rather than on paper qualifications.

For the provinces, harmonization was seen as involving too much of a federal set of intrusions. Moreover, education was an area of provincial jurisdiction. As a result of this impasse the federal government changed its position and supported the preferred provincial option, which centred on the concept of mutual recognition. This was, to put it simply, the 'driver's licence' model. Provinces simply accept and recognize the qualifications as certified by the another province. Some provinces such as Quebec also cited the example of the European Union in this regard, where mutual recognition was the approach taken. An initial federal draft containing this approach became, with amendments, an Alberta draft and started a process towards consensus which all provinces could work from.

With regard to licensing and the linked issues of professional qualifications, the problems went beyond the issue of standards versus mutual recognition. In labour areas such as the building trades, regulation was directly carried out by the provinces. Hence, programs such as the Red Seal program on the apprentice trades had been worked out to enhance mobility. But, as mentioned, the professions were governed by various kinds of self-regulation. The rationale for self-regulation was that the province would stay out of the way of the professions in terms of expert qualifications, provided they behaved in the public interest. But the implications of the labour-mobility chapter was that now the provinces would be telling them what to do largely because Ottawa was saying so. Indeed, in some provinces, including Ontario, the pressure in recent years had been to agree to self-regulating status for more and more occupational or knowledge groups.

Since the professions were the main new ground in which the federal government in particular wanted to extend mobility rules–based concepts, it is useful to digress somewhat to discuss the nature of self-regulation in these realms. There is an extensive literature on the regulation of professions, but our examination of it must be extremely brief.

There are four central principles or questions inherent in regulating professions (Slayton and Trebilcock 1978; Bayes 1986). The first centres on the nature of the service involved. Professional–client relationships involve a highly individualized form of service geared to the client's specific needs and circumstances. The service also involves a technically sophisticated base of knowledge. And it involves extensive realms of professional judgment applied to specific case situations. Other key dilemmas of regulation flow from these service and relational characteristics.

The second issue is that normal competitive markets as a 'regulator' and traditional direct regulation by the state are both virtually impossible to employ in these circumstances (Trebilcock 1983a). Normal markets are difficult because there is no homogeneous product whose price will provide appropriate market relations and signals. Each output or service is unique. For the same reason no regulator or regulatory commission can specify outputs and standards as a basis of direct regulation. It follows as well that clients of the professional service provider must place a considerable amount of trust in the integrity and competence of the professional. Society, on the other hand, through its political institutions, will not likely allow unfettered trust. Trustworthiness will somehow have to be shown, that is, 'regulated.'

A third issue of principle flows out of the trust relationship. It is that a professional culture and set of entrenched norms and principles must be developed collectively by the profession though education and other ongoing mechanisms. But individuals, and individualism, may break these norms. The client must have almost perfect information about professional suppliers, a condition which rarely applies, and hence which supplies one of the most broadly supported rationales for government regulation.

A fourth principled concern goes beyond service outputs and relates to the quality of outputs (Dewees 1983). Quality is not a simple concept in that it could be an attribute related to price or the basic absence of value for money. Quality can also extend to characteristics of technical ability, including such things as the ability to explain things clearly to a layperson.

Given these characteristics, only certain kinds of regulatory mechanisms or models become available, and these initially involve choices about regulating inputs versus outputs. Each has different advantages and disadvantages, only some of which are highlighted here. One method of social control is the judicial regulation of outputs through a civil-liability suit for professional negligence. It can be directed at a particular output, and is often quite a flexible and non–state-interventionist approach. But it is a system that must be initiated by the victim, and has other problems associated with costs and the suitability and knowledge of the courts.

A second output-based model is to attempt the direct regulation of outputs. Despite the arguments above that this is extremely difficult, it has certainly been present for some professions, such as chartered accountants. Such regulation involves the establishment of some form of specialized administrative agency, and accordingly has an array of advantages and disadvantages, including potentially greater informality of approach compared to the courts, but also potential 'capture' by the profession and problems of credibility.

As for input-based professional regulatory models, there are essentially two: certification and licensure. Certification essentially involves an agency or authority certifying to the public that certain ('registered') individuals have the requisite competence and training. Uncertified individuals are not barred from supplying services in this regulatory model.

In contrast, a system of licensure involves a regulatory arrangement whereby only licensed providers are allowed by law to practise. Unlicensed service providers can be prevented from practising, and thus disciplined by the state, directly or indirectly. As is the case with certification, licensure systems make the often extremely questionable assumption that there is a tight link between the inputs (education and training) of professionals at time 'a' (when they are certified or licensed) and outputs (an array of decisions on specific cases over many years – time 'x,y,z').

It is only after puzzling out the above array of service characteristics and input versus output regulatory choices that one can then add the further choice – namely, should the state then regulate directly or should it delegate regulation to the profession? This is the model referred to as 'self-regulation' but which is in fact delegated regulation. The key here, not surprisingly, is that, in professional knowledge and service-delivery realms, the central relationships of 'agency' are dual in nature: first, between the professional and the client, and, second, between the profession and the state.

To the above regulatory brew one finally adds federalism and mobility issues *per se*, and the battle over a standards/competencies approach versus a mutual-recognition approach. It is little wonder that the provinces adopted a go-slow tactic. It is also not surprising that this sectoral table, in contrast to many others, did undertake a consultation process. But it was mainly the federal government that led the consultation, largely through the national associations of various professions.

Three briefing and consultation sessions were held in April 1994. Participants from thirty associations attended, and another seventeen were kept abreast of the developments in the negotiations. The associations ranged from those for lawyers, doctors, engineers, and accountants, to those for technicians, technologists, and para-professionals. The federal negotiating team regarded these consultations as valuable and found broad support for the general direction they were taking, though also for a 'go slow' process of change. This may have been simply because they were national associations rather than the provincial self-regulating bodies and professions themselves.   .

The provinces in general did not undertake their own consultation with provincial bodies, although they did have a reasonable sense of the issues that the latter would raise. The final agreed-upon approach in the chapter was an extensive work program whereby the provinces would engage in discussions with their various professions with a view to making changes that would enhance mobility.

The chapter also specifies quite a wide range of 'legitimate objectives' ultimately linked to the public-interest and trust issues discussed above, but also reined-in by disciplines so that, when these are pursued, they are not done in way that creates disguised restrictions to mobility.

The labour-mobility chapter was much more of a federal-versus-provincial battle, and the final trade-offs reflected the fact that the federal government was the main demandeur. The federal government achieved a set of mutually stated obligations, an extended scope to the mobility rules, and a work plan to keep up momentum on the professions. The provinces achieved their preferred mutual-recognition approach rather than the harmonized-standards approach with some room for local job initiatives.

Environmental Protection

Key Provisions

When seen as a trade-related issue, environmental-policy matters typically centre around the need to solve two problems (Esty 1994; Appleton 1994). The first is how not to lose business, trade, and investment due to such activity moving to jurisdictions with lax environmental policy or enforcement – in short, to one or more rogue jurisdictions. The second problem is how not to lose control over environmental laws due to downward pressure on standards and standard-setting. Canada's trade and environmental policy makers had just struggled with these issues in the NAFTA environmental side-deal negotiations. The concern there was that Mexico's environmental laws and enforcement were a problem in both these respects. But because the gap was so great, the strategy was not to harmonize laws immediately, but rather for Canada and the United States to offer technical assistance to enable Mexico to close whatever gaps there were.

In the Canadian internal-trade context, the above dual problems were still at the centre of the issue, but the gap in capacities among provinces was not as great in the NAFTA–Mexico context. Hence the focus in the negotiations was on harmonization but with a view to ensuring strong environmental standards and enforcement. The chapter contains a general undertaking in Article 1508 that the parties shall endeavour to harmonize environmental measures that may directly affect internal trade following principles set out in two previous federal–provincial agreements. The agreement is also to strengthen existing levels of environmental protection and not to lower those levels. Nor can parties offer to waive or derogate from its environmental measures as a way to attract or retain business.

The chapter also makes clear that each party has the right to establish its own environmental priorities and levels of environmental protection and can maintain differing standards. The wording of the agreement also encourages the parties to continuously improve levels of environmental protection.

Negotiating Dynamics and Issues

The environmental protection chapter was negotiated by an ad hoc working group of the strategic planning committee of the Canadian Council of Ministers of the Environment (CCME). The CCME was thought to be the best vehicle for negotiations because its ongoing work on federal–provincial harmonization was initially seen as being perhaps all that would be needed for an internal-trade exercise (Doern and Conway 1994; Boardman 1992). The CCME also had a well-established secretariat in Winnipeg and had extensive avenues of contact with the environmental non-governmental organizations (ENGOs).

The federal negotiator was the director of the Federal–Provincial Relations Branch of Environment Canada, and the provincial negotiators had all been through the ups and downs of recent federal–provincial environmental policy making. When dealing with one another, the environment officials often had quite difficult relationships over jurisdiction and duplication in implementation, but when faced with economic departments and interests within and among their own governments, they were quite capable of uniting against the common foe.

As the negotiations began, many of the players had been involved in finalizing the NAFTA side agreement on the environment, which had itself been an afterthought to NAFTA proper. It had been forced on to the international-trade agenda by the then newly elected Clinton Administration and had been a welcome second chance for both federal and provincial green policy makers to get environmental matters more firmly recognized (Doern 1993).

With the NAFTA experience fresh in their minds, there was very little difficulty in getting the CCME group, chaired by British Columbia, to agree that their objective would be to ensure that the AIT was at least as green as NAFTA. Indeed, the group quickly came to see the environmental protection chapter basically as a way to guarantee the ability to implement measures on environmental protection within the larger internal-trade agreement. This environmentally led objective was aided by the realization that there was little reliable research on precisely which environmental measures were in fact barriers to internal trade. If one did not know what barriers there might be, then it followed that one could not engage in a process of eliminating or reducing them. The 'eliminate/ reduce' logic, however, was the driving force of the internal-trade negotiation as a whole.

The main tension in the environmental negotiations was reflected in the early drafting process. Initial drafts in January 1994 came from B.C. and Ontario, both NDP-governed provinces. They cast the environmental chapter as horizontal, and thus prevailing over all other parts of the agreement. This kind of thrust was in keeping with the late 1980s and early 1990s positions of most environmental-policy makers in that, under the banner of sustainable development, they saw this framework commitment as crucial (Toner 1995). Indeed, the federal government and other G-7 governments had committed themselves to ensuring that all government policies would be assessed according to whether or not they advanced the goals of sustainable development.

The negotiating team also took this stance in pure bargaining terms · since it knew that the pressure from the other tables would be to water this down. This expectation quickly materialized in the form of a second draft chapter submitted by the Internal Trade Secretariat. Three features of this draft were crucial. First, it covered all environmental measures whether or not they affected internal trade. The environmental table countered by seeking to narrow the scope to only those environmental measures that directly affected internal trade. Second, it included a provision intended to prevent the lowering of environmental protection as an inducement for investment. The environmental table agreed with this change. Third, the second draft also emphasized that regulations and standards had to be based on risk assessment and scientific proof. The table countered here by insisting that there be a provision that recognized that the precautionary principle could be used as justification for environmental measures even where the scientific evidence was not conclusive.

These key issues were augmented by other more particular issues and terms in the agreement. These issues in turn reflected an array of differences: among provincial environmental participants at the sectoral table; between the environmental table and other tables; among departments within each province; and interdepartmentally within the federal government.

An initial issue was the early use of the term 'ecosystem integrity.' This was the initial phrase to emerge from the environmental table intended to capture the breadth of sustainable-development concerns and values. But the economic departments of all governments, including Natural Resources Canada and Industry Canada's federal negotiators, argued that they were just getting used to, and were perhaps even understanding, the meaning of the term 'sustainable development' but were now being hit with yet another concept. As a result, the term 'environment' was used, but reference was also made to 'interacting systems.'

Like all chapters in the agreement, the environment chapter had to accommodate its own version of exceptions. The battles over scope were a part of this, but so also was the issue of the right to maintain 'nonconforming' measures. Some provinces pushed for a virtual open-ended right. But, in the end, pressures from the main negotiating table resulted in the inclusion of a NAFTA-like provision which gives the parties two years to identify non-conforming measures and then a commitment to 'endeavour to develop' a work plan to eliminate those provisions by the start of the year 2000.

A third area of contention centred on the nature of the provision on the prohibition on lowering environmental standards. By referring to 'standards,' this provision carried with it the potential of making it impossible to alter some standards, even where new scientific and technical evidence indicated that alternative means could be used to obtain the same level of protection. As a result, the wording was changed to prevent the lowering of levels of environmental 'protection.'

The above differences seem innocuous, but in fact were central to a much larger debate among traditional environmentalists who preferred prescribed command and control approaches, and economists and trade experts who preferred economic performance-based criterion (McFetridge 1990). They differed in how compliance should be approached in social regulation. Environmental performance standards specify a given performance criterion, such as a particular reduced level of pollution emission (hence, the protection required), and then prefer to leave it up to the polluter as to how it will go about achieving the result. In principle, this allows the polluter to take action with least-cost methods suitable to that firm's or industry's particular production and market situation. The alternative is to define standards, not in output terms, but in terms of how they must be maintained. This specification of the means in a design sense is viewed as being doomed to inefficiency and unfair enforcement since it imposes uniform solutions to many different kinds of production situations. In environmental and occupational health areas, this design approach often is revealed by regulatory requirements either for the best practicable or available technology or for more particular kinds of equipment (e.g., installing scrubbers). In recent years, the latter approach has come to be viewed as command-and-control regulation, while the former is seen to be an example of the more beneficial use of regulation based on economic incentives or market approaches (Benedickson, Doern, and Olewiler 1994).

Needless to say, the proposal that the environmental protection chapter take precedence over other chapters raised serious concerns in other tables and among the chief negotiators. In the end, environment as a fully horizontal chapter was not to be. The compromise suggested by Ontario and agreed to was that the agreement would contain a general commitment to take environmental considerations into account. Moreover, the preamble to the agreement contains a commitment, among many others, to promote 'sustainable development and environmentally sound development.' Thus, the environmental protection chapter is undoubtedly horizontal in its subject matter, but it is not horizontal in its precedence over other vertical chapters where inconsistencies exist. Article 1501 indicates simply that, when there are inconsistencies with another chapter, the parties shall endeavour to reconcile the inconsistency.

A final provision where differences arose centred on dispute-resolution panels and their environmental expertise. The environmental table initially proposed that a separate roster be established for disputes involving environmental matters to ensure that the right expertise was brought to bear. The main table saw this as being too cumbersome and, in the end, a provision was agreed to that enables the use of environmental experts at all stages of dispute resolution, including conciliation and mediation, as well as on relevant panels.

The environmental table was also cautious about how easily one went to the panel stage. Environment Canada was especially concerned that contentious disputes in one area did not side-swipe other areas where environmental cooperation was good. Thus an emphasis on conciliation and cooperation was more in keeping with the way it was hoped that environmental federalism would evolve.

While the above account may indicate unusual unanimity within the table between the federal government and the provinces (in the face of the common economic ministry sceptics), there was always, beneath the surface, a strong difference that had to be managed and contained. This was that the provinces, in their overall green agenda, tended to focus on administrative transaction-cost problems. There was too much overlap between the two levels, and thus, on harmonization matters, the provincial logic tended to argue that the federal government should simply back off. The federal government's position was also a twofold response that defended its jurisdiction and the politics behind it. First, federal jurisdiction was fully justified, at a minimum because of transboundary issues, and at a maximum because of globalization concerns and commitments. These issues could not be handled by some kind of 'club of provinces.' Second, federal environmental-policy makers had ample evidence to support their view that the ENGOs trusted the federal government on green matters far more than they did the provinces.

The federal position in the environmental table was also taken with a firm eye on what was feasible within the federal government. Environment Canada knew that it was the federal internal-trade people in Industry Canada who were leading the negotiations. On the other hand, the Minister of the Environment during the period was Sheila Copps, who was known as a strong defender of the federal environmental role and of tough environmental enforcement measures. A middle position between these two views was needed.

Among the provinces, environmental sympathies also varied. Within the table, Alberta took the hardest line, in keeping with its view that this was basically an internal free-trade deal. B.C. was a strong supporter of the environmental components but also came to use them in the end-game in a dispute with Newfoundland linked with investment provisions. It will be recalled from chapter 4 that, at the end, Newfoundland sought a wide array of regional exceptions to the agreement. In these final battles, B.C. threatened to use the dispute-settlement provisions of the agreement to ensure that Newfoundland's pulp-and-paper mills were complying with environmental measures and were not using non-compliance as an investment advantage.

Given their considerable lobbying influence, it is surprising that the ENGOs were not more extensively involved in consultations with the environment table. During the negotiations, the federal environment negotiator met with only two groups and received submissions only from the Canadian Environmental Law Association and the West Coast Environmental Law Association. This was in part due to a lack of time in the early months of 1994, and in part due to the previously noted general strictures against elaborate consultation processes that had come down from the chief negotiators.

In the overall scheme of things, it would appear that the sectoral table's goal of getting an environmental chapter that was as green as NAFTA was probably achieved. But, as was the case in NAFTA, it is also in some sense a side deal in that few gains were made. For the environmental-policy makers, the internal-trade negotiation was just one more arena in which to carry the environmental agenda. The federal–provincial harmonization agenda has been the subject of negotiations since. On 31 May 1996 the Canadian Council of Ministers of the Environment, whose role was further entrenched by the internal-trade agreement, announced an updated set of governing principles centred on issues of harmonization (Canadian Council of Ministers of the Environment 1996).

Conclusions

The above examination of the three sectoral negotiations convey some of the different negotiating processes, dynamics, and institutions that are inevitable in a multi–policy field negotiation being carried out under the rubric of internal trade. Our sample of sectoral tables in this chapter is skewed in that each of the sectors involved areas that are horizontal in nature. Investment, labour mobility, and environmental protection were all seen as aspects that cut across all of the vertical sectors of the economy.

None of the above three horizontal framework areas succeeded in being a horizontal chapter that totally took precedence over other chapters. They do, however, all have *some* aspects of supremacy over other chapters. This was the natural outgrowth of the inner tension in the negotiations between those who saw it as, first and foremost, a trade negotiation, and those who saw it as primarily a negotiation in which other values about governance and legitimate objectives should either prevail or occupy appropriate policy and political space in the Canadian federation.

In two of the three areas – investment and labour mobility – the federal government was undoubtedly the demandeur, arguing for a principled, rule-based approach versus a 'listing and solving' of barriers approach, as preferred by most provinces. The federal government found allies for its views mainly in Alberta and Manitoba but also considerable opposition headed by Ontario, B.C., and Saskatchewan. The sectoral tables also reveal many more subtle particular positions from various provinces, as would be expected in complex sectoral situations.

The inward tentacles of NAFTA and GATT and their attendant liberal trade ideas were evident in the sectoral tables, especially in the investment regimes being advocated, and in some respects in the environmental chapter. The labour-mobility chapter had fewer immediate international-trade links *per se*, although the example of the European Union had resonance in the debate regarding the preferred approach of mutual recognition of occupational qualifications as opposed to full harmonized standards. The labour-mobility table was also without doubt the table that had the least experience with trade-like negotiations, since this area had been entirely a domestic federal–provincial field.

The degree to which each sectoral table was tied to the central politics of the chief negotiators' table varied. Each table, of course, had some connection as the deal was hammered out, but the investment table in particular was bound up, especially because of the links with procurement and regional-development policies. The labour-mobility and environmental tables had somewhat greater independence, in part because they were functioning within, and being negotiated by, quite well-established federal–provincial policy communities and institutions.

There was also a sense in both these tables that strategies were different. The environment table was not a federal-versus-provincial battle, but rather it involved a process whereby the environmental negotiators saw themselves in common cause against the trade community, and hence sought to preserve recent NAFTA gains regarding the recognition of sustainable development without being swamped by a trade-oriented negotiating juggernaut. The labour mobility table was also tactically limited in that in many respects this was the first full-scale negotiation on labour mobility, especially regarding the professions, and hence there was a sense of making progress simply by getting key issues recognized.

The three tables also varied in the extent to which they involved outside interest groups. As we have seen, the general stricture in the negotiations as a whole was to keep discussions confined to officials and ministers. The investment-chapter negotiators stuck to this approach, although, given the NAFTA/GATT agendas, where business contact was frequent and recent, formal consultation may not have been necessary.

In the case of the environment chapter, the contact with ENGOs was remarkably small, especially given the great vigilance of the ENGOs. Some consultation did occur, however.

It was in the labour mobility chapter negotiations that consultation with interests was most in evidence. This was undoubtedly because the professions were involved. Interestingly, this consultation was federally led and involved national associations rather than the more influential provincial self-regulating entities and professions themselves.

7

Sectoral Negotiations III: The Agricultural and Food Goods, Resource-Processing, and Energy Sectors

We turn now to the AIT negotiations in the natural-resource sector writ large. This area of the economy and of federalism involved three different sectoral negotiating arenas which in total dealt with agricultural and food goods; mining; forestry; the fisheries; and the energy realms of oil, gas, and electricity. The chapter examines the negotiations in the context of three separate tables of negotiators, but it is important to see the natural-resource sector writ large as well.

The areas of mining, energy, and forestry alone in 1992 accounted for 42 per cent of Canadian exports, and constituted 14 per cent of GNP, 8 per cent of employment, and 25 per cent of investment (Natural Resources Canada 1993). Agriculture is a crucial resource in every province, but is a dominant part of the provincial economy in provinces such as Saskatchewan and Prince Edward Island. The fishery has major importance in Atlantic Canada as a whole, and Newfoundland in particular, and also in British Columbia. Oil and gas as a resource base are the life blood of the Alberta economy, and crucial to Western Canada as a whole. Mining and mineral resources drive the northern hinterland regions of every province, but especially Ontario, Quebec, British Columbia, and the two territories. Forestry is a key engine of the B.C. economy, but is also an important sector in each province (Natural Resources Canada 1994). And, finally, all the resource sectors have been increasingly linked to the issues of sustainable development and the environment.

It is also important to stress that the resource sector has historically been embroiled in key aspects of national-mythology and federal–provincial politics (McDougall 1986; Scott 1976; Richards and Pratt 1979). The central aspect of national mythology is that Canada's economy has lived off its resources and taken them for granted, causing the national psyche to avoid facing the hard realities and inadequacies of other aspects of the economy, including manufacturing, and science and technology. Resource ownership and jurisdiction over resources have been central to many federal–provincial political disputes (Doern and Toner 1985; Drushka 1985; Anderson 1985).

In fact, as we will see, jurisdictional aspects have always varied within and across the subsectors. Agriculture is an area of explicit concurrent jurisdiction under the constitution. The fisheries have also had shared jurisdiction. The ownership and management of resources in the mining, forestry, oil, gas, and hydro-electric sectors is firmly in provincial hands, but the federal government has jurisdictional roles regarding exports and interprovincial trade. The politics of the resource sectors have also been linked to a strong east–west or central-Canada-versus regions political dispute (Nelles 1974; McDougall 1982). Much of this emerges from the initial National Policy of the 1870s, when high tariffs were erected to protect Ontario and Quebec manufacturing but also resulted in resentment in the resource-feeder regions, especially in Western Canada, but also in Atlantic Canada. A more recent point of intense resentment centred around the federal Liberal government's 1980 National Energy Program, which Western Canada, and Alberta in particular, saw as a resource and tax grab by eastern governments, consumers, and voters at the expense of the Western resource producer (Doern and Toner 1985). The subsequent Mulroney government's reversal of these policies in the mid-1980s and in the Canada–U.S. Free Trade Agreement of 1988 won widespread support in Western Canada (Toner 1986; Doern and Tomlin 1991a).

As will be seen, the starting point for defining each sectoral table is the primary resource itself, but each table is then immediately embroiled in how far along the production chain it can go in defining the limits of free-trade federalism. In the agriculture table, the issue is immediately joined because the table already included the food-goods sector as well as primary agriculture producers. In the resource-processing table, the focus was to be on the subsequent processing of any given resource into goods and value-added products, but the key question was 'to what point and how far?' At the energy table, where a chapter failed to be agreed upon, some dispute emerged over energy-related services, but the table failed to get a deal, largely because of the issue of the interprovincial movement or 'wheeling' of electricity.

The format for our brief account of each sector is fairly straightforward. For each sectoral table and chapter, we first set out the key provisions in the AIT. We then describe the key dynamics and issues in each table. In the conclusions, we look across the three negotiating and policy tables as a whole.

Agricultural and Food Goods

Key Provisions

The provisions in Chapter 9 of the agreement cover all agricultural and food goods except fish, fish products, and alcoholic beverages. Article 901 specifies that, if there are inconsistencies between the sectoral chapter and the general rules, the Chapter 9 provisions prevail to the extent of the inconsistency.

The influence on the sector by the agricultural policy community is also revealed by the provisions in Article 902, which states that the agreement applies 'only to measures identified as technical barriers to trade by the Federal–Provincial Agri-food Inspection Committee.' The technical barrier is defined mainly to include a measure that: (1) involves product characteristics or their related production methods; (2) deals exclusively with terminology, symbols, packaging, and marking or labelling requirements; and (3) involves a sanitary or phytosanitary measure. There is also a provision for the inclusion of such technical measures 'with policy implications' to come within the agreement effective 1 September 1997, after appropriate review.

The sanitary or phytosanitary measures are of course crucial 'health and safety' regulatory measures, but the parties are enjoined by the agreement to ensure that, when proposing such measures, they take into account the implications of such measures for internal trade. The parties also agree that their measures will not 'arbitrarily or unjustifiably' discriminate between parties, nor constitute a disguised restriction on internal trade.

However, the key areas left for further review are those which deal with the sensitive issues of supply management and safety-net programs for agricultural producers. Article 903 commits the parties to 'reduce or eliminate measures that constitute obstacles to internal trade,' but this is to be done in the context of a review with no apparent deadline, and in the context of Canadian agri-food policy as a whole. The three areas mentioned in Article 903 are: the development of sustainable orderly marketing systems in the dairy, poultry, and egg industries; the Western Grain Transportation Act; and federal and provincial agricultural safety-net programs.

The Negotiating Dynamics and Issues

The confined nature of the agricultural chapter must be seen in the context of the evolution of federal and provincial agricultural and food policies in the 1970s and 1980s (Skogstad 1987, 1992, 1993), an area of concurrent jurisdiction under the constitution. During the 1970s, the federal government administered the main programs in income and price supports and had the dominant research expertise (Gilson 1989; Prince 1990). The provincial governments implemented extension programs, but they also had primacy in many areas of technical regulation (Haack, Hughes, and Shapiro 1981). In the early 1980s, this pattern changed, primarily through the addition of numerous provincial price and income-support programs. By the mid-1980s there was a growing recognition that the internal market in agriculture was quite balkanized. In the latter half of the 1980s, the federal government devoted much of its policy energy into trying to reorder agricultural policy so that there was a greater semblance of a national (as distinct from a federal) policy (Menzie 1988; Prentice 1994).

However, layered into this policy and political mix was the debate about, and the negotiations involved successively in, the FTA, NAFTA, and the GATT–WTO Uruguay Round. These stretched over the entire 1986–95 period. The FTA in particular had a major impact on agriculture (Doern and Tomlin 1991a, ch. 5). Its key provisions were the elimination of tariffs over then years and the prohibition of export subsidies on bilateral trade with the United States. The FTA protected the Canadian supply-management system and its various marketing boards. The FTA was the first trade agreement to subject agriculture to GATT-like rules, and it was negotiated amid considerable tension between primary agricultural producers and food-product manufacturers (Skogstad 1995a; 1996). The new tensions centred basically on the fact that Canada's food-product manufacturers would increasingly have to face competition from U.S. manufacturers whose input costs were lower, largely because the United States had a more market-based or non–supply-managed system. In the FTA, the supply-management system was preserved, due to the superior political power of the primary producers, but the seeds of major change had been planted nonetheless (Doern and Tomlin 1991a; Skogstad 1993; 1994).

The later NAFTA and WTO agreements extended the trade-based tentacles of policy further into domestic agriculture/food policy and program realms. The changed relationship between the two overall interests, primary producers versus food-products manufacturers, was also reflected in the restructuring of federal ministries in 1993, when Agriculture Canada became Agriculture and Agri-Food Canada (Agriculture and Agri-Food Canada 1995).

Supply management was not the only big-ticket problem on the agri-food agenda. Also present was the continuing debate about the Western Grain Transportation Act. Based on subsidies that link back to the historic Crow's Nest Pass Agreement freight rates, this debate centred on the economic distortions created in the grain-transportation system (Harvey 1980). Thus, in the agri-food sector, barriers to internal trade were clearly both federal and provincial in nature and origin.

The negotiations that produced the agricultural and food goods chapter also occurred in the more immediate context of earlier discussions in the agricultural policy community about internal trade as such. First, academic analysis had indicated the balkanization and some of the adverse competitive impacts by categorizing barriers under headings such as transportation, subsidies, and other policies and regulations (Haack, Hughes, and Shapiro 1981). It also pointed out related national-unity issues. Second, in their joint National Agricultural Strategy of 1987, ministers of agriculture agreed to reduce barriers to trade, and the Federal–Provincial Agricultural Trade Policy Committee (FPATPC) was given the task of identifying and dealing with the barriers.

This review showed that, among the eleven governments surveyed, there were up to 158 measures that affected interprovincial trade in agriculture. It also showed that there was considerable dispute as to whether and to what extent these measures may or may not distort interprovincial trade (Federal–Provincial Agricultural Trade Policy Committee 1988). This 1988 report eventually led to the December 1989 Memorandum of Understanding (MOU) signed by ministers of agriculture. A further MOU was agreed to in November 1992.

When the broader internal-trade negotiations of 1993–4 began, the ministers of agriculture had, in essence, already agreed to:

– undertake collective action to reduce or eliminate barriers;
– a best-effort moratorium on the introduction of new barriers;
– provide information and the opportunity for consultation when any new regulation is under consideration that might affect internal trade;
– identify barriers as prime candidates for further work; and
– establish a formal mechanism that would include binding dispute-resolution processes.

In all of the above prior work and thought, the focus was still basically on technical barriers to trade. The larger supply-management and grain-transport issues were the most significant barriers, but they also required a different political arena from an internal-trade negotiation for discussion and resolution. In 1995 the grain transportation issues were in fact dealt with when an array of transportation subsidies were abolished as a deficit-reduction measure.

At the sectoral table in 1994, the federal government and Alberta were the primary advocates of a maximum removal of barriers. This was also a sector, however, where British Columbia was quite supportive as well. The discussions tended to centre around the federal government and Ontario, Quebec, and Alberta, in part because they had the largest expert bureaucracies in the agricultural policy field. In a negotiation that focused on technical barriers, this was of considerable importance.

But beyond this initial clustering of provinces, it is important to appreciate that every province had sensitivities and concerns regarding its provincial poultry, egg, and dairy producers (Skogstad 1990a). The provincial horticultural producers and lobbies were also important. These concerns are also strengthened by the fact that representation in provincial legislatures is not strictly based on a full 'representation by population' basis, but rather has a 'rural tilt' that is significant inside legislatures and cabinets.

A province such as Saskatchewan, moreover, had concerns about whether an extensive internal-trade agreement would in some way harm or undermine federal institutions such as the Canadian Wheat Board (Skogstad 1995b). More particularly, it was concerned that at some future date products such as canola might not be able to be marketed in a similar fashion if internal-trade rules went too far in a free-trade direction.

The flavour of the negotiations in the agricultural and food goods sector was also affected by the obvious fact that federal policies were the source of barriers. This was true not only in areas such as the Canadian Wheat Board and grain-transportation, but also because agriculture was a concurrent power, and hence both governments could and did act with new initiatives over the years. Unlike in some other sectoral tables, the federal government was thus not free to be 'above the battle' since it, too, was a part of the problem (Prentice 1994).

In the early stages of the negotiations, a majority of provincial governments argued for the simple acceptance of the 1992 MOU as the agricultural and food goods chapter and that this be done without adopting the general rules of the internal-trade agreement as a whole. Alberta, B.C., and the federal government strongly opposed this position for four reasons. First, progress in eliminating barriers had been slow. Second, there were no firm deadlines. Third, there was dispute as to whether the MOU included those technical barriers with policy implications (see more below). Fourth, there was no effective dispute-resolution mechanism.

The negotiations almost immediately focused on several technical barriers with policy implications. Policy implications simply meant that they were controversial in some major recognized sense and had been on the agricultural agendas for several years. These technical regulations included: provincial regulations on margarine colouring; the reintroduction of the 'No. 1 small' potato grade; standards for butter blends (mixtures of butter and margarine) and imitation dairy products; the movement of fruit and vegetables in bulk containers; and provincial regulations for fluid milk production and distribution. Several agriculture ministers did not want to see these issues handed over to, or dominated by, an interprovincial internal-trade policy process.

There were also a far larger array of other technical barriers (i.e., those with no, or much less, policy controversy attached to them). Technical barriers involve regulations that require producers from other jurisdictions to change the preparation of their product for sale in the local provincial market, such as through changes in grading, labelling, packaging, or the content of ingredients (Prentice 1994). These can increase both the cost and the risk of trading for outside producers from other provinces. The negotiations on technical barriers initially centred on just how fast different provinces considered they could respond, and how sensitive particular standards might be to producer groups in their province. The other fault line in the negotiations centred on the provisions regarding scope and review, and hence on what items, if not decided now, would have to be decided over a three-year period, by 1997.

In the final two meetings of ministers of agriculture, consensus emerged around the provisions described above, especially the elimination of all the purely technical barriers, but also the inclusion of firm undertakings, with deadlines, to eliminate the technical barriers with policy implications. Importantly, there was also a commitment to a moratorium on any new barriers.

The dispute-resolution provisions were not particularly contentious. There was pressure from the federal government and Alberta for a greater use of the general agreement provisions on dispute resolution, but this was not strongly pressed. Agreement quickly emerged that the sectoral chapter dispute-resolution provisions had to be used and exhausted first.

It is obviously important to ask how the earlier (and partially concurrent) international-trade agreements and/or international-trade pressures affected the negotiations in the agriculture–food sector. It would appear that the effects were not from the FTA, NAFTA, and the WTO agreements as such, but rather from the indirect impact these were already having on the economy, and then on ministers of agriculture and on their now much more complex and interwoven political constituencies in the agri-food sector.

One effect, already apparent even at the 1992 MOU stage of consideration, is that ministers were much more aware of the competitiveness aspects of their decisions and of the rationalization of production that was already occurring. Agricultural policy could no longer be made in a vacuum, ignoring international considerations. A second effect, particularly after NAFTA, was the embarrassing recognition that foreign jurisdictions and their firms had, in some instances, better 'national treatment' access to Canadian provincial markets than some Canadian provincial producers and firms had. This is because international-trade agreements set the standard of national treatment at the level of the best province in terms of liberalization and lack of barriers.

A third effect came in the debate in 1994 (and since) at the agriculture–food table about the need for national technical standards. As we saw in the labour-mobility sectoral negotiations, the overall free trade–internationalization dynamics meant that Canada could not offer up ten different sets of technical standards for dozens of products or groupings of products. The provinces knew change had to occur, but they also did not want national standards to be *federal* standards.

The choice here was expressed as between a harmonization option and one involving recognition of equivalents. Harmonization was the choice arrived at, but this did not eliminate debate or controversy. For example, efforts had been mounted to develop a national dairy code, but by definition a 'code' is not harmonized. Moreover, there are many specific dairy products to accommodate. Similar problems confront the previously mentioned issue of imitation dairy products. Should harmonization be at the level of principles only, or actual performance/quality standards? Does one need a special set for subclasses such as cheese-based products?

A final aspect of the 1994 negotiating process is the issue of interest-group involvement. There was some brief canvassing of interest-group views through the use of the international trade-based SAGIT on the agriculture and agri-food sector. Some forms of surrogate interest-group input also occurred for the food-goods producers through Industry Canada, even though the food manufacturers' previous sector branch in Industry Canada had gone to Agriculture and Agri-Food Canada in 1993. But largely, the ministers of agriculture were able to keep the negotiations to their arena of decision making, not only because of the limited time available for the negotiations, but also because they were confident that their departments had good functioning antennae tuned to their respective interest-group and product-group organizations and contact points.

Natural Resources Processing

Key Provisions

Chapter 11 of the AIT contains the provisions regarding the 'processing of natural resources,' defined in Article 1102 as 'the production and sale of the forestry, fisheries and mineral resources products listed in Annex 1102.2.' As was the case with agricultural and food goods, in any inconsistency between Chapter 11 and other chapters, Chapter 11 prevails.

The chapter also specifies that the agreement does not apply to: (1) the licensing, certification, registration, leasing, or other disposition of the rights to the harvesting of forestry, fisheries, and mineral resources; (2) the management or conservation of forestry, fisheries, or mineral resources; (3) water, and services and investments pertaining to water; or (4) other measures listed in Annex 1102.3 (see more below).

Under Article 1103, the parties agree to consult each other in order to remove barriers that are causing significant harmful economic effects, and they agree to use the chapter's own dispute-resolution processes before resorting to that of the AIT as a whole.

A Working Group on Processing of Natural Resources is also established that will undertake reviews to assess whether the chapter has met its objectives; to resolve implementation issues; to revise the chapter in the future; and to assess opportunities for progress on items not covered in or excluded by the agreement.

Negotiating Dynamics and Issues

The negotiations at the table on the processing of natural resources were

co-chaired by Alberta and B.C., largely out of strong provincial government views that a federal chairing role was inappropriate, given provincial ownership and control of natural resources. The fishery was the only
exception to this, and the federal players at the table included a representative from Fisheries and Oceans Canada, which at times functioned
like a federal player and at times like a quasi-provincial resource owner.
The federal role was otherwise concentrated in the considerable expertise of Natural Resources Canada (NRCan) which encompassed the
forestry and mining sectors (Doern 1995). Other NRCan officials were
involved in the separate energy sectoral table (see more below).

The provincial negotiators typically came from provincial natural-
resource ministries, where there was considerable expertise about the
resource sectors as a whole and the various provincial policies and regulations governing them within each province. The federal government,
through NRCan, arguably had more product-specific knowledge than the
provinces typically had, a fact which affected some of the issues regarding
the scope of the final chapter.

The fact that the chapter/table was called the 'processing' of natural
resources rather than simply 'natural resources' was decided at the political level quite early on. In part, this was intended to give the chapter
more substance in internal-trade terms while showing that the control of
natural resources as such was still unambiguously provincial. But this
could never solve the ultimate problem of where the conceptual boundary of the primary resource ended and 'processing' began.

It was around this central issue that most of the negotiations centred.
Quebec and Saskatchewan were particularly adamant that a very narrow
construction be put on the boundaries – in effect, somewhere between
extraction or harvesting and secondary or further processing. Alberta,
Manitoba, and most of the Atlantic provinces pushed for broader coverage.

The federal negotiators sought as broad coverage as possible. They
started from a premise that products listed in the common customs
nomenclature of FTA/NAFTA and related international-trade product
categories should be used. The provinces baulked at this kind of breadth.
In concert with the Industry Canada–centred federal negotiating view,
the NRCan officials sought a resource and resource-processing sector
that was as efficient and competitive as possible and assurance that any
firm in the economy that needed access to the resource could obtain it at
an efficient and competitive price.

In the early stages of discussions, the tension over the boundaries for processing produced many examples where one or another province suggested cut-off points such that, for some firms and plants, the line was drawn literally *within* the plant. This was analogous to saying, for example, that processing would cover pulp but not paper or not particular paper products (e.g., wallpaper). Eventually, it was agreed through the listed Annex 1102.2 products that processing would cover any fishery, forestry, or mineral and metal product which could be produced in the same processing plant that carried out the primary processing.

Another early issue regarding the scope and coverage of the chapter concerned water. Ontario wanted to include water, resource-related services, tourism, and waste management as issues for coverage. Water had been a political controversy in the FTA negotiations, particularly for the NDP, and thus the Ontario government was concerned (Doern and Tomlin 1991a; Hart 1994). Like the FTA provisions, it was fairly quickly decided that water would be defined very narrowly and that, except for containerized water, it would be excluded from the chapter and from the AIT as a whole. Other linked issues, such as tourism, were left as subjects for future review.

Beyond these general dynamics, there were other more particular issues regarding exemptions. From the outset B.C. made it known that it would oppose any item that could affect or set precedents regarding the need for the province to preserve its existing controls over the interprovincial export of unprocessed logs. These controls were a part of B.C. forestry law passed in the late 1940s, which B.C. believed had been grandfathered under GATT. But there were in 1994 fresh legal concerns that they may be challengeable under GATT. Both the United States and Japan had been opposed to B.C.'s controls. Thus B.C. was insistent that nothing be done in the AIT that might potentially affect this larger issue.

It must be remembered that the bases for provincial control of their resources is an array of either, or both, export and entry rules, licences, and regulations. Thus the B.C. logs issue which was declared exempt from the chapter had parallels for other provinces. Newfoundland wanted to preserve controls regarding the export of unprocessed fish. Alberta and B.C. had a dispute at the time regarding the control of logs. Quebec also sought to exempt fish and logs. The federal government also sought exemptions, especially one regarding fishing licences.

In a more general context, all provinces wanted an exemption for their overall function of the management of the resource, activities which included conservation and the allocation of harvest quotas. These in turn were contentious regarding other chapters in the AIT, on labour mobility and on investment. As the final chapter agreement shows, B.C. and Alberta got exemptions regarding unprocessed logs, and Quebec and Newfoundland received exemptions for unprocessed fish. An effort to include a provision to finally resolve these at a later date was dropped.

While the above issues and dynamics were central to the negotiation table, there were other inter-table and intra–federal government controversies at play. NRCan members along with Industry Canada participants in the federal strategy saw that the greatest gains for the resource industries and firms they were concerned about would come from removing the barriers imposed by other federal departments and provincial departments. In this regard, attention focused on the environment, transportation, labour mobility, and investment issues. In short, attention had to be paid to several of the other sectoral tables and their chapters. NRCan's sectoral impact analyses saw these, in effect, primarily as a factor of production for the resource and resource-processing and product-producing firms.

The most contentious issue was the activities of the environment table. The resource-processing table as a whole saw the environmental table as having an extremely aggressive agenda which was seeking to have the environmental provisions dominate other sectoral provisions. The negotiators at the resource-processing table were especially concerned about the advocacy of the precautionary principle in environmental regulation, including its implications that conclusive scientific evidence need not be present. Within the federal government, several NRCan and Environment Canada meetings took place around these issues. There were also crucial concerns about the potential primacy of the environment chapter's dispute-resolution processes and that the resource industries would in effect have to resolve disputes in an environmentalist-designed final dispute-resolution process. In the end, as we have seen in chapter 6, this level of environmental dominance simply did not prevail.

In the chapter on the processing of natural resources, there are particular items to clarify these environment-related sensitivities with greater certainty. One provision (Article 1102.4) ensures that an environmental measure is defined as *not* including the management or conservation of fisheries resources. Article 1105 also ensures that criteria for environmental measures must include 'a reasonable level of scientific and technical evidence.'

Energy as the Missing Chapter

In chapter 4 we have already sketched out, in the context of the overall negotiating dynamics, why there was a one-paragraph energy chapter, or in effect a missing energy chapter. In the current context of our look at all of the resource areas (agriculture, forestry, fisheries, and mining), energy deserves a somewhat closer, albeit still brief, examination. The short version of the energy story already told in chapter 4 is that, in the oil and gas sectors, there was already close to full internal free trade. It was the electricity sector that posed the problems, especially issues regarding the wheeling of electricity between provinces, where a controversy between Quebec and Newfoundland was particularly troublesome. Alberta was not prepared to see an energy chapter included until all energy sources were included.

Not surprisingly, the full story of the energy non-chapter was more complicated than this. Alberta chaired the energy table, and the energy negotiators at the official level sought in good faith to have an energy chapter. A draft chapter at the early stages had garnered support for the general proposition that the chapter apply to all energy goods and services. This, however, would be subject to a basic 'notwithstanding clause' which would exempt provincial monopolies. Attention then turned on how to constrain these entities to some extent in a pro–internal free-trade direction.

Saskatchewan and Ontario were strong supporters of preserving their monopoly rights for gas and electricity transmission and distribution, and provincial rights to regulate these activities. At the other end of the continuum, Newfoundland sought full rights to the wheeling of electricity, including binding dispute-settlement provisions. All other provinces, led by Quebec and Ontario, thought that wheeling and transmission access across provincial boundaries were issues best left for their electrical utilities to negotiate. There was a very real political imperative to this deference. Hydro utilities were big players in provincial economies, and, moreover, it would be a brave energy-table negotiator who would dare take on the hydro CEOs, who were of course major political appointees in those provinces with provincially owned monopolies (Daniels 1996).

The federal government could not play a role in electricity from a position of real strength. It did not own hydro utilities, nor have to finance or guarantee their debts. It broadly supported the view that there be open internal trade on all energy products, but it also had to be careful that it did not take sides in the Quebec–Newfoundland dispute over electricity.

In the end, there was no energy chapter, but there was a commitment that energy-chapter negotiations would be extended until 30 June 1995. Subsequent meetings were held which allowed more direct involvement by the hydro utilities and which focused on which particular kinds of access and wheeling might be allowed.

In the end-game of the 1994 ITA negotiations, the energy chapter was taken off the table by ministers. Electricity wheeling across provincial boundaries was undoubtedly the crucial issue, but there were also other underlying concerns about intraprovincial electricity trade. The hydro utilities were facing many changes that were altering their accustomed and relatively stable lives as regulated public utilities (Vollans 1995). These included technological changes and co-generation options; relative and inter-fuel costs and pricing choices of a more complex nature; declining economies of scale; and so-called stranded investment assets or overbuilt capacity.

These changes produced different permutations and combinations of concern in different provinces. For Ontario and Quebec, it was the inherent magnitude of what to do with giant utilities and bureaucracies such Ontario Hydro and Hydro-Québec. For Saskatchewan, there were concerns that, if it was connected to an interprovincial grid, its internal, relatively high-cost, power would or could be supplied by Manitoba or Alberta (both lower-cost producers). For Alberta, its bullish position on free trade in electricity was premised in part on the fact that it already had an intraprovincial grid that it felt could be the model for Canada. P.E.I. had a vested interest in freer electricity trade because it was dependent on electrical power from New Brunswick and believed it could get cheaper power from Quebec.

Newfoundland, as we have seen, refused to sign an energy chapter largely because of the wheeling issue. But it was also fiercely critical of its fellow provincial negotiators in that, in Newfoundland's view, they lacked the determination to reach a Canadian decision but would likely have to soon reach the same free-trade decisions because of U.S. rules. The U.S. pressure to do so was largely emerging from rulings by the U.S. Federal Energy Regulatory Commission (FERC). Its rulings regarding Regional Transmission Grids (RTGs), which Canadian utilities would be a part of, would forbid one member of the grid from discriminating against other members of the grid. In effect, internal free trade for electricity in Canada would become a made-in-the-U.S.A. policy.

Conclusions

The natural-resource aspects of the AIT were negotiated in three sectoral tables. Each sought in its own way to advance internal trade, but always in the context of quite deep-seated concerns about provincial control of most natural resources. The agricultural and food goods table achieved advances in the realm of technical standards, but only by ensuring that the larger barriers found in supply management and transportation were not dealt with in an internal-trade political forum. The table dealing with the processing of natural resources struggled over where to draw the line regarding products that were close to the primary resource and those that were farther up the value-added production chain. Progress was made in reducing barriers, but again there were enormous sensitivities regarding the provinces' powers over resource ownership and control. The resource-processing negotiating group also spent a considerable part of their negotiating efforts fending off the feared incursions of the environmental table.

The energy table ultimately failed to produce an energy chapter because of sensitivities regarding the interprovincial wheeling of electrical energy. But it was also weighed down by the considerable problems felt by many provinces regarding not only how to manage intraprovincial electricity trade, but also how to deal with the very real political power and prestige of provincially owned utilities.

8

'Rules about Rules,' Dispute Resolution, and Institutions

The dispute-resolution and institutional provisions of the AIT are set out in Part V of the agreement and were clearly the object of major discussions. In chapter 4, we have already provided an initial account of some of these provisions, but only generally in the context of the main end-game trade-offs of the main table negotiations. The resulting patchwork quilt of dispute-resolution provisions reflects again the collision between the two overriding visions of the deal – as a trade agreement and as a governance-of-federalism agreement.

In this chapter, we look more closely at the content of these provisions and the negotiating processes surrounding them. But first we need to bring together some issues regarding the extent to which the AIT is itself a set of 'rules about rules' because of the way in which it attempted to fashion agreement around issues of regulation and standards. These are examined in the first part of this chapter. In the second section, the key provisions on dispute resolution and institutions are profiled briefly. In the third section, we look at several key aspects of the negotiations. The fourth section looks briefly at the first major case to test aspects of dispute resolution, the dispute between British Columbia and New Brunswick regarding the consolidation of United Parcel Service (UPS) customer-service operations into one operation in New Brunswick as an alleged violation of the agreement and the investment chapter's incentives-code provisions. In the fifth section, we examine the links between dispute settlement, the agreement as a whole, and the debate about the federal trade-and-commerce power.

Rules about Rules? Standards and Regulatory Measures as a Horizontal Issue

As we have already seen from the analysis of sectoral negotiations in chapters 5, 6, and 7, there were various ways in which the general issue of standards and regulatory measures came to the fore in the AIT. Thus an important question in an overall institutional sense is whether the AIT does establish some rules about rules. Standards can be seen as just another kind of rule or regulation (delegated legislation), but they are also seen, as becomes apparent below, as a separate realm (Jacobs 1995; Michael 1996). In the context of free-trade federalism, they raise issues of preferred framework regulatory principles such as mutual recognition, harmonization, and performance-based regulations and standards whose origins are increasingly found in international-trade and related agreements, but which play out differently in domestic politics. As mentioned, we have already encountered these issues in the discussion of the labour-mobility, and agriculture and agri-food sectors. But in these areas there were separate negotiations about standards and regulatory measures on their own.

Building on earlier discussions from the late 1980s and early 1990s, the AIT negotiators were given several principles by ministers to work from. One of these was that governments reconcile standards and regulations to provide for the free movement of people, goods, services and capital within Canada. In the earlier stages of the AIT negotiations, the reconciliation of standards was considered to be the purview of a separate team focusing on consumer-related measures and standards. However, it quickly became evident that standards crossed many sectoral aspects of the AIT process and needed to be negotiated by a separate group that would look at the issue comprehensively. In the final agreement, this produced Article 405 and two annexes (405.1 and 405.2), on standards and standards-related measures, and regulatory measures, respectively.

Article 405 enshrines the principle of reconciliation, which the parties agree to support. However, reconciliation, given the need to leave room for legitimate objectives, is deemed to mean many things. It can mean 'mutual recognition,' where the requirements of the provinces are equivalent in purpose and effect. It can also mean harmonization, which itself is seen to be a broad concept ranging from compatibility to full convergence.

In the early stages of negotiations, the federal government pushed for a view that mutual recognition should require all parties to the AIT to accept relevant standards-related measures as equivalent to their own until they can supply a sufficient explanation as to why they should not. Several provinces strongly objected, arguing that such an approach could work only if measures are equivalent in purpose and effect. Many feared that such a concept could ratchet standards in a downward direction, and hence harm legitimate objectives. The federal government backed off its aggressive initial stance, apparently to ensure that a separate annex on regulatory measures could remain in the AIT.

Harmonization was also a contentious concept. The federal government sought harmonization with international standards and with harmonization obligations in international-trade agreements. Within the country, the federal government also tended to see harmonization through the creation of national standards. As we have already seen, the provinces were not well disposed to these views, and in particular saw harmonization as a reciprocal arrangement between affected provinces.

In the negotiations two other contentious issues emerged. The first was whether the article should or could apply to goods as compared with services and investment. Ontario, in particular, saw services and investment as more complex economic activities and that hence no single generic concept was sufficient. Both stayed in the agreement, but in separate clauses, since the federal government pressed hard for an encompassing approach to goods, services, and investment.

A second area of contention was whether Article 405 should apply to regulatory measures as well as to standards. Many provinces objected on the grounds that 'regulatory' potentially applied to any measure that a government might introduce, and hence would extend too far into provincial jurisdiction. As a result, a separate annex was agreed to, which, among other things, commits the provinces to a best-efforts approach to addressing the reconciliation of regulatory measures, including those which do not contain a standard. Annex 405.2 is therefore grounded much more in a consult-and-cooperate approach than is Annex 405.1 on standards.

However, Annex 405.1 also reveals the need for compromise, as the negotiators sought to balance trade-centred rules with the legitimate objectives of governance in the Canadian federation. Thus, the annex applies only to those standards included in the scope of the sectoral chapters. Concerns were also raised that private-sector standards-development organizations might create internal-trade barriers. The annex requires governments to make such bodies aware of the governments' obligations under the AIT.

In the discussions over standards, there was apparently quick agreement that performance standards rather design standards should be used. In other words, standards should be based on what products or services must be able to do (performance) rather than specifying how they should be structured or required to operate procedurally (Laplante

1990; Michael 1996). Once again, however, this agreement was not as clear-cut as it seems, in that provinces could interpret the principle in varied ways. Performance criteria could be used unless it could be demonstrated they would not achieve a legitimate objective. A performance approach had to be considered among many alternatives. Or such an approach could be used to the extent it was appropriate and desirable.

Other provisions of Annex 405.1 centre on the issue of rationales and science-based standards (and regulations). Some parties pressed for language that stated that there must be a scientific or factual basis for a standard. In the end it was agreed that there had to be a 'reasonable' basis for the standard. The federal government also sought to include criteria for assessing risk similar to those in GATT and NAFTA. These criteria were dropped, and only a vague 'where appropriate' reminder was left in as an adjunct to the 'reasonable basis' criteria set out above.

Finally, the annex on standards contained provisions on conformity assessment. The intent here was to facilitate reconciliation by assessment of conformity, but also to ensure that conformity-assessment procedures are not themselves used as disguised trade barriers. Conformity assessment is deemed in the AIT to include a range of obligations, from the use of equivalent conformity-assessment bodies, through the recognition that different procedures can produce equivalent results, to the avoidance of multiple testing procedures.

The AIT reflects an effort to supply a general approach to standards and regulatory measures, but the negotiations clearly reflected strong differences of view as trade versus governance values and criteria were brought to bear. The standards chapter, moreover, was linked to an array of consumer-related measures which we have not covered in the discussion above (Hadfield, Howse, and Trebilcock 1996). But, just as importantly, it was played out in practical terms in several other sectoral regulatory fields.

The Key Provisions on Dispute Resolution and Institutions

The provisions on dispute resolution are contained in Chapter 17 of the agreement. An overall principle of cooperation is set out as the guiding norm since the parties 'undertake to resolve disputes in a conciliatory, cooperative and harmonious manner.' This includes the use of other dispute-avoidance and -resolution processes. Article 1701 also indicates at the outset that the dispute-settlement processes apply to the interpretation or application of the agreement.

TABLE 2

The Two Main Internal-Trade Dispute-Resolution Processes

Government-to-Government	Person-to-Government
Consultations	Initiation of proceedings
Assistance of committee	Screening
(including ADR processes)	Consultations
Request for panel	Assistance of committee
Establishment of panel	(including ADR processes)
Panel report	Request for panel
Implementation of report	Establishment of panel
Non-implementation	Panel report (possible award
· Publicity	of costs of proceedings)
· Retaliatory action	Implementation of report
	Non-implementation
	· Publicity

There are three overriding aspects to the dispute-settlement process. The first aspect is crucial but can be briefly stated – namely, that parties must use the dispute-avoidance and -resolution processes in the applicable sectoral *chapter* before they can use the provisions in Chapter 17. These various chapter-based processes are also listed in Annex 1701. The second and third aspects contained in Chapter 17 cannot be briefly stated. They deal with government-to-government processes, on the one hand, and person-to-government processes, on the other. They are summarized in table 2, and each is briefly discussed below.

A quick glance at table 2 shows that the two processes have many common stages of progression, including: consultation; assistance of the committee (within which there are several possible alternative-dispute-resolution [ADR] processes); a panel stage; panel report implementation; and non-implementation provisions. Table 2 also shows that the person-to-government process is somewhat more elongated in the initial stages and truncated at the end. The main difference is that, in the early stages of the person-to-government process, there is a screening stage. An independent screener is required to be appointed by each party to ensure that private actions are not vexatious or of a harassing nature. The truncated feature at the end is largely due to the fact that publicity is the only real 'sanction,' since retaliatory measures are not allowed, nor is the award of damages. Only costs of proceedings *may* be awarded by a panel.

It must be reiterated, however, that these two stages 'kick in,' in most cases, only *after* the chapter-specific route has been exhausted.

These chapters also contain several consultation, ADR, and other dispute-avoidance and -resolution processes.

Each of the stages in all processes is accompanied by specific provisions for time and deadlines, or at least minimum and maximum potential time configurations. The intent is to ensure cooperative but also expeditious decision making about disputes. As we see below, in the discussion of the UPS case, the full process can be much longer than the 180-day maximum period for international-trade dispute-resolution processes under NAFTA.

To understand the dispute-resolution processes more precisely, one must quite literally deal with the detailed sector chapter and Chapter 17 provisions. Space does not permit us this kind of detail here, but several other features of the process can be highlighted in a more general way:

– The consultations are confidential.
– The committee-assistance stage centres around the Committee on Internal Trade but also typically includes other sectoral committees mentioned in various chapters.
– Panels are composed of five members drawn from a roster maintained by the parties to the agreement. Each disputing party appoints two panellists from the roster who were not nominated to the roster by that party. The appointed panellists then select the chairperson of the panel from the roster.
– All proceedings before a panel are public, but all documents filed are accessible only to the parties.
– The provisions for retaliation in the government- to-government 'non-implementation' stage allow the complaining party to suspend benefits of equivalent effect or, where this is impractical, impose retaliatory measures of equivalent effect against the party complained against.

The overall dispute-resolution processes and provisions must also be linked to the institutional provisions of Chapter 16. The above-mentioned Committee on Internal Trade is composed of Cabinet-level representation from each party. Its main tasks are to supervise the implementation of the agreement and to assist in the resolution of disputes. The Internal Trade Secretariat is also established (based in Winnipeg), funded 50 per cent by the federal government and 50 per cent by the ten provincial and two territorial governments on a pro-rated basis. Also established is a working group on adjustment to assess the effects of the agreement on each province in each fiscal year.

While these are the central overall institutions established *by* the agreement, they are by no means the only institutions *of* internal trade. As shown above, and in our analysis of sectoral negotiations in chapters 5, 6, and 7 of this book, there are also sectoral federal–provincial committees that are involved in chapter-based areas. Moreover, within the federal government and within provincial governments, there are many line departments and central agencies also involved as disputes or issues or work programs wend their way through thirteen governments.

The Negotiating Dynamics and Issues: A Closer Look

The negotiations on the dispute-settlement and institutional provisions saw a broadly similar pattern to those traced in chapter 4 for the negotiations as a whole. The federal government and Alberta pressed for a full binding dispute-settlement regime. Ontario, B.C., and Quebec formed an alliance that called for a broad consultative approach only. The other jurisdictions fell somewhere in the middle, with Saskatchewan being the most opposed in this group to any binding system.

The potential models for a dispute-settlement system had been examined in a 1992 study for Industry Canada (then Industry, Science and Technology Canada) and included approaches based upon recent trade agreements (FTA, NAFTA), European Union approaches, and adaptions of existing federal–provincial approaches. Also drawn upon were the then emerging approaches towards alternative dispute resolution (ADR), which were seen as more cost-effective ways of handling many areas of regulatory compliance. EU approaches were briefly considered, but concepts such as the use of a judge advocate or similar adapted institution were seen as too foreign to the Canadian and North American legal systems.

The federal government had suggested that dispute settlement be linked directly to a permanent Internal Trade Committee that would be federal–provincial in make-up, that would be headed by a high-profile person, and that would directly appoint and manage dispute-settlement panels and related machinery. The key opposing provinces quickly rejected this idea, arguing that provinces were sovereign entities within a system of federalism and that no enforcement mechanism should be ceded to a powerful 'third tier' institution, nor to the courts. Nor, many key provinces argued, should the federal government be the arbiter of disputes.

The discussion of models quickly settled on some aspects of the dispute-resolution provisions built into Chapter 20 of NAFTA and Chapter 18 of the FTA, but structured in such a way that it was clearly government driven and controlled rather than private-sector-access driven. Moreover, the structure of dispute resolution was also sealed by some of the key decisions taken very early on in the process regarding the primacy, or lack thereof, between horizontal principles and vertical or sectoral chapter rules.

The main impact here, as we have seen, was that, in dealing with disputes, parties are first driven to the sectoral chapters, and hence to the specialized line (or sectoral) departments, for the first stage of dispute resolution. Here they must first go through the steps of alternative dispute-resolution (ADR). Only then can they proceed to the next level, which is the 'trade' or industry department level. And only after that is there a possibility of panels. Thus the system is quite paternalistic and designed to have many checkpoints where the governments can snuff out a controversy or cut it off entirely, or, perhaps resolve it. In short, it was intended to make panel-based dispute cases rare and exceptional because of the prevailing view among many provinces that, in Canadian federalism, the norm should be that governments can work things out in good faith.

The dispute-settlement provisions were negotiated in three meetings with ministers. At the first meeting the basic parameters were set. Ministers ruled out access to the courts, a special tribunal, or any other type of permanent institution. In the second meeting, ministers were basically 'walked through' the steps and then asked to decide which approach to take. This is the process that led to the three-step concept: ADR, specialist department consideration, and then the trade department step and possible panels. A third meeting focused on the crucial issues of enforcement, including the issues of retaliation. It was Alberta that forced the pace on this key issue by threatening to walk away from the negotiations if there was not some kind of reasonable private-action provisions. The remedies for private action, however, are very limited in that there are no retaliation provisions, only limited cost awards possible and, ultimately, a reliance on negative publicity as a sanction.

In the discussions on dispute-resolution, the federal government and Alberta sought to ensure that the dispute-resolution processes were seamless, with no unilateral default points, that is, stages at which any one party could prevent the next stage from occurring. This was achieved, *except* for the panel stage, where a province can simply not appoint its suggested panel members.

Internal-trade ministers as a whole had concerns similar to those of their senior officials about the dispute-resolution provisions. Ministers were especially concerned, however, about liability issues and damages that governments might have to pay, and, as mentioned, there was a strong view that the courts must be avoided.

There was little or no direct private-sector involvement in the dispute-settlement negotiations as such. Major business associations had been calling for a good enforceable agreement but did not get very specific about actual mechanisms. The only other contributor to the dispute-settlement discussion during the negotiations was Professor Michael Trebilcock of the University of Toronto, who conducted a seminar for the negotiators on various dispute-resolution mechanisms. As a result of criticism launched at the seminar, panel proceedings, which were seen to be private, were opened up to some public scrutiny.

Indeed, it could be argued that the dispute-settlement negotiations were characterized by a fear among many provinces that they would be harassed by aggressive interest groups and associations. The majority of provinces wanted to insure that umbrella organizations could not band together. Accordingly, in the private-access provisions, it is made clear that only persons or companies with a direct interest would have access. At the insistence of Ontario, a provision was included that defined a labour union as a person for purposes of dispute settlement. It was also on this basis that the position of 'screener' was established to help root out frivolous challenges or cases.

The United Parcel Service Case and the Dispute-Resolution Process

Early in January 1995, United Parcel Service (UPS) announced that a consolidation of most of its customer-service functions would occur and would result in the relocation of 870 jobs (but not necessarily personnel) from B.C., Manitoba, and Ontario to New Brunswick. This happened after the signing of the internal-trade agreement in July 1994, but before the agreement took effect on 1 July 1995. The UPS case immediately became the first test of the dispute-resolution process, particularly regarding the code of conduct under the investment chapter.[1] Thus we first

---

1 As this book went to press, a further case went to a panel review. This was the manganese-based fuel additives issue. Alberta took on the government of Canada, alleging that federal law banning the use of the additive violates the AIT. Ironically, it pitted against each other the two governments that were the strongest supporters of the AIT on an issue involving federal legislation. The panel ruled against the federal government.

present a brief chronology of the UPS case and then an examination of the key issues it raises.

UPS indicated in January 1995 that its move to New Brunswick was due to the latter's favourable business climate and its sophisticated telecommunications facilities. Indeed, New Brunswick premier Frank McKenna's avowed industrial strategy had focused on the telecom-centred service area. In the UPS case, New Brunswick had provided about $6 million to UPS through training-assistance grants and a forgivable loan.

The then B.C. minister of employment and investment, Glen Clark (who later became premier), expressed public concern to the media about the case and was critical of New Brunswick. He vowed to take action under the Agreement on Internal Trade. It is worth remembering from earlier chapters that, although Clark took a highly combative approach to the negotiations, and B.C. only reluctantly signed, one of the key areas of B.C. interest was the investment code of conduct and the need to prevent investment poaching.

The B.C. Minister then immediately wrote to New Brunswick requesting information under Article 10 of the agreement (Annex 608.3) dealing with the 'Code of Conduct on Incentives.' B.C. also approached federal industry minister John Manley, in his capacity as co-chair of the Committee of Ministers on Internal Trade, and twice requested an immediate meeting on the matter. The response was that this was premature in terms of the dispute-resolution process.

The New Brunswick Minister of Economic Development and Tourism replied to the B.C. inquiries by arguing that the incentives supplied to UPS predated the AIT's coming into effect and, moreover, were not contrary to the code, and that he was not in a position to discuss proprietary, company-specific information. In late February 1995, B.C. then requested that consultations among officials take place and pointed out that appropriate information had still not been supplied.

The next stage of the case involved the CMIT. In April 1995 the issue was discussed *in camera*, but the only result was that officials were asked to do some analytical work regarding the issue of the consolidation of operations in one province and whether paragraph 4 of the 'Code of Conduct on Incentives' (Annex 608.3) applied. There then followed a series of exchanges in which New Brunswick argued that the CMIT had exonerated New Brunswick, with both Minister Manley and B.C. arguing that the CMIT had made no such decision.

It was not until early October 1995 that B.C. and New Brunswick officials met for formal Article 614 consultations. These were still under way in April 1996, at which point a frustrated B.C. sought formal consultations under Article 1702 (the general dispute-resolution provisions). In June 1996, B.C. indicated to the Committee on Internal Trade that it may soon request its assistance in resolving the dispute. Meanwhile, the committee had suspended its work on interpreting the consolidation issue pending the resolution of the UPS case.

By the latter part of July 1996, B.C. had formally requested the assistance of CIT. New Brunswick's response was that B.C.'s complaint should be dismissed on the grounds that the UPS measures were authorized before the standstill period under the Agreement on Internal Trade came into effect. As evidence of this position, New Brunswick sent the CIT a copy of a letter dated 14 January 1994, outlining the terms of the incentives being offered to UPS.

By the end of the summer of 1996, the CMIT was reluctant to proceed itself because it had insufficient information, this time about whether the standstill period had been violated. From January 1995 to the end of August 1996, some 20 months, or more than 600 days, had passed without yet getting beyond the 'assistance of committee' stage. No panels had been created since, to date, B.C. had not requested that any be established. There was also concern that, even if a panel was requested, New Brunswick might be able to stop the panel stage in its tracks by refusing to appoint its panellists.

For its part, New Brunswick also believes that, at the actual AIT negotiations in 1994, consolidations of plants were not covered by the code. Otherwise, New Brunswick argued, a 'have-not' province could never attract firms who might, for very good reasons, want to consolidate operations. After more and more information was exchanged between B.C. and New Brunswick about the case, New Brunswick increasingly felt that B.C. was treating it not as a fellow province, but rather as a mere party in a dispute. Increasingly, it argued that 'enough was enough.' New Brunswick was also critical of the internal-trade ministers for their failure to take responsibility. In particular, New Brunswick pointed to other features of the dispute-resolution process which required ministers to decide through a consensus. By late 1996, New Brunswick's view was that there was no case to resolve. In 1997 the case had fizzled out, with B.C. apparently concluding that it did not want to pursue it through any of the really definitive formal AIT channels.

The UPS case is only one, but it did raise several issues that are endemic to dispute resolution. The first, of course, is the nature of the dispute itself. Was New Brunswick's incentive package simply one that reflected a sound industrial strategy aggressively carried out? New Brunswick, it could be argued, has simply found the remaining limited crevices in the fine art of attracting investment. For a 'have-not' province, trying to become a 'have' province, are there no incentives that are allowed? The spectre of a rich province like B.C. taking on a poorer province seems contrary to a least some of the spirit of federalism, but, then again, all provinces did agree to discipline themselves through the agreement and through the code on incentives. Indeed, such a code is at the heart of the politics and substance of the agreement.

The second issue in the UPS case concerned the matter of interpreting the agreement on both the 'consolidations' issue and the standstill issue. The latter is undoubtedly a short term problem in that UPS simply crossed over the start-up phase of the agreement. The issue of consolidations is more difficult, since such corporate choices will undoubtedly occur quite frequently, especially in the light of modern telecommunications and service-delivery possibilities.

A third issue is that B.C. immediately sought to skip stages by going public and then going to the Committee on Internal Trade. B.C. of course, agreed to the dispute-resolution steps in the agreement, but it is clear that the complaining party may itself quickly become impatient and seek other political avenues of resolution.

The fourth issue is inextricably linked to how long a dispute-resolution process could take. Since this depends on the exact sectoral chapter that might be involved, it is hard to describe any typical time-line. If all went well, in some processes it could take up to 270 days. Others could take well over 400 days, from the chapter-based start-up process, to a dispute that resulted in retaliation following a government-to-government dispute where the party complained against had not implemented a panel report. The UPS case could have taken up to 800 days (the time spent to the end of 1996), plus possible future stages, if it had been fully pursued.

In general, both the UPS case and the broader analysis above suggest that any assessment of the negotiations about dispute resolution must look at the structure of the entire agreement. There is no statement of the primacy of the freedom of goods in general. The structure of the chapters of the agreement had been settled on very early, when a list of issues was assembled which more or less became the chapters. For those used to an international-trade-agreement structure, the mixture of horizontal and vertical chapters was like a bad dream.

More than anything else, it is this matrix structure which drives the start of the dispute-settlement process to the sectoral chapter provisions first, and hence lengthens dispute resolution considerably.

Dispute settlement is also ultimately affected by the other key architectural features. The concept of legitimate objectives is turned on its head compared to a trade agreement. In a regular trade agreement, the general concept is that governments can pursue general public-interest objectives provided that there is national treatment – namely, that such policies are not constructed so as to discriminate between national and foreign firms. In the internal-trade agreement, rather than providing a rationale for enacting non-discrimination measures, the legitimate-objectives provisions allow the parties to avoid the non-discrimination requirements.

Dispute settlement is also affected by the large number of exemptions, including federal exemptions. The exemption for culture is wider in the internal-trade agreement than in NAFTA in that, in the former, it includes both culture and cultural industries. In the internal-trade agreement, the exemption for regional development starts with language similar to that in the WTO–GATT document but then permits, as chapter 5 showed, broad decentralization initiatives, a provision Quebec insisted be in the agreement. Banking and financial industries are also exempt at the insistence of Ottawa and the Department of Finance.

Dispute Resolution and Debates about the Federal Trade-and-Commerce Power

Discussions about an internal-trade agreement have always been couched in differing views about several related federal powers under the Canadian constitution, including initially conferred powers such as the 'peace, order and good government' and 'trade and commerce' powers. They are also linked to provisions under the Charter of Rights and Freedoms regarding mobility rights (section 6) which, along with other charter rights, are constraints on the powers of both levels of government. The dispute-resolution provisions were inextricably tied up in these debates because they would ultimately do most to define how far actual federal powers might extend. The fact that the Agreement on Internal Trade was not to involve the courts, and hence was a political agreement, is also germane. So also is the provision in the AIT that the agreement is not supposed to change the constitution.

With respect to the 'peace, order and good government' and the 'trade and commerce' powers, the courts have generally favoured a narrow interpretation. In the realm of the trade-and-commerce power, this has meant that the federal government has had 'very little scope to enact national legislation where divergent provincial regulatory approaches undermined the Canadian economic union' (Howse 1996). The 'peace, order and good government' powers were largely confined to national emergencies.

Recent legal analyses suggest that the courts in the 1990s are giving more scope to these federal powers. For example, in the General Motors case, the issue of the constitutionality of federal competition law was involved (Howse 1996). Competition law had been centred historically on federal powers over criminal law, but, especially since the 1986 Competition Act, federal powers were based on the trade-and-commerce provisions, in part because more civil matters based on economic criteria of anti-competitive behaviour were involved (Doern 1995). These could collide with provincial jurisdiction over property and civil rights. In the General Motors case, the court activated the little-used 'general regulation of trade' dimension of the trade-and-commerce power (Howse 1996). In these and other cases, issues related to the securing of the economic union have been expressly a part of court judgments.

Thus there is certainly some basis for arguing that the trade-and-commerce power, alone or in combination with other powers, gives more federal scope for action. Howse's recent analysis brings out, however, other necessary points of caution. He suggests that a national regulatory scheme is not likely to 'simply pre-empt provincial laws but normally will operate concurrently with them' (Howse 1996, 12). Thus cooperation with the provinces would be necessary in any event since, otherwise, such federal exercises may simply create another layer of barriers to internal trade because of the added regulatory complexity. This potential would depend in part on whether the doctrine of paramountcy would apply. If it was applied, paramountcy would be given to federal law.

Constitutional aspects of the internal-trade agreement are also found in section 6 of the Charter of Rights and Freedoms. It provides for the right of Canadians to reside and gain a livelihood in any province subject to general 'reasonable limits.' A key limitation to this power is that it does not apply to corporations, and also there are some court decisions which suggest that this does not confer a right to 'earn a livelihood independent of some element of mobility,' in short, a move to take up residence in another province (Howse 1996, 8).

Prior to and during the internal-trade negotiations, the debate on the trade-and-commerce power inevitably raised its head, especially in relation to contemplating strategies regarding dispute settlement (but also regarding the agreement as a whole). The trade-and-commerce power, as set out above, gave the federal government jurisdiction over interprovincial trade in *goods*, but the extent of this jurisdiction over other issues, such as services and capital, and the extent to which the power could be actually exercised had always been circumscribed by the legal uncertainties already mentioned, but also by political realities.

As a result, during the internal-trade negotiations and the preparations for them, there were voices within the federal government and within the lead department, Industry Canada, which were arguing that the federal government should aggressively exercise such powers and test them to the limit. Equally, there were other voices which advocated extreme caution.

Legal opinions were obtained by the Justice Department, which expressed considerable confidence that the federal government did have the jurisdiction to enact laws to secure the 'four freedoms' of an internal common market: the freedom of people, goods, services, and capital to move and do business within Canada without discrimination.

But politics usually dictated that the federal government could never fully play the trade-and-commerce card because of the political conflicts it would create with the provinces. Some effort to do this had been part of the Meech Lake and Charlottetown constitutional discussions, but these had ended in failure. They had largely failed because of their collision with provincial desires to practise some form of regional (provincial) economic-development policy. However, opposition was also expressed on more general political grounds, especially in the case of Quebec, but also by all provinces.

The trade-and-commerce issue was therefore a kind of unspoken presence during the negotiations. It was known that the card could never be fully played, but it was also possible that if a successful internal-trade agreement (and its dispute-resolution provisions) did not in fact work, then a future federal government might well conclude that it had to be more aggressive because, after all, it had tried all the alternatives. However, at the same time, Article 300 provides that nothing in the agreement alters the legislative authority of Parliament or of provincial legislatures.

The combined effects of the dispute-resolution provisions and the 'matrix' trade-agreement structural concoction referred to above are such that judgments vary about whether the agreement enhances or constrains the federal government's trade-and-commerce power. Those who think that it has constrained the trade-and-commerce power fear that it has set limits around the power, and that the courts, using doctrines of 'constitutional convention,' may simply conclude that what is practised (namely, the internal agreement as a living document) is what the constitutional trade-and-commerce power in fact is. Since the trade-and-commerce power has never been fully defined, the agreement is what will define it.

The alternative line of argument is that federal trade-and-commerce powers are in fact enhanced by the agreement because it is the discriminatory power of provincial governments that have been most reined in. Many actions that provinces previously did take are simply less and less possible.

Conclusions

The negotiations on standards and regulatory measures, dispute resolution and institutions, and the final content of these provisions, each reflected the shadowy grey zone in which the participants sought to place the agreement. It was a side deal to the constitution, but it was not supposed to change the constitution. It was a political agreement that was intended to avoid the courts, but it was also to be implemented in good faith. In much the same way that many regulations and guidelines in government are seen to be the outcomes of 'negotiating in the shadow of the law,' the Agreement on Internal Trade and its dispute-resolution provisions are the product of negotiating in the shadow of the constitution.

Regarding standards and regulatory measures, we have seen that some jurisdictions sought to enshrine international trade–derived principles and concepts, including mutual recognition, harmonization, performance-based regulation, and science-based regulation. The final AIT shows that, though progress was made in this overall direction, there is by no means full agreement on 'rules about rules,' and indeed that several provinces resisted these concepts when cast in a domestic context and when advocated by a federal government whose overall agenda many provinces were suspicious of.

The dual dispute-resolution avenues – government-to-government and person-to-government – were designed by governments and for the convenience of governments. Though the dispute-resolution procedures are said to be based on a spirit of cooperation, it is equally possible to say that their elongated nature is based on the fact that the governments did not fully trust each other, and trusted private interests and interest groups even less.

But these complex processes are also due to the nature of the negotiations themselves and to the architecture of the agreement. Above all, it was the matrix architecture of the agreement itself which forced the first stages of dispute resolution into the chapter or sectoral realm. The agreement is thus a bastardized trade agreement, if the norms of an international-trade agreement are applied. But it is also a bastardized federal–provincial agreement if 'normal' federal–provincial relations is the criterion of assessment.

These complex features are also why assessments vary about whether the agreement and the dispute-resolution features enhance or detract from the federal government's exercise of its trade-and-commerce powers, and hence its lead role in the enhancement of the Canadian economic union.

9

Conclusions

The broadest purpose of this book has been to examine the main issues and contours of free-trade federalism in Canada, primarily through an account of the negotiation processes in 1993–4 that produced the Agreement on Internal Trade (AIT) between the federal government and the provinces and territorial governments. It has also sought to provide an initial assessment of the processes and institutions involved in the AIT and the prospects for their future adaptation in Canadian free-trade federalism. Such an assessment centres on the broader institutional aspects of policy making through multi–policy field trade-like negotiations in the realm of federal–provincial relations.

We began by stressing that free-trade federalism is both an old and a new subject. It is a subject of old importance because, when the Canadian federation was formed, the rationale for creating a federal political structure was in part the establishing of an internal common market or economic union. Free trade within such a union tended to be seen as the free flow of goods and the absence of tariffs. Free-trade federalism is also a subject of new or refurbished importance, in the last decade in particular, because of global and national developments that range from the impacts of free- or liberalized-trade agreements such as the FTA, NAFTA, and the GATT–WTO Uruguay Round, to the internal stresses of possible Quebec separation, the latter based on promises of political sovereignty coupled with free trade with the rest of Canada.

How then does one view Canadian free-trade federalism as a new century emerges? One way is to have clearly in mind a picture of what the bedrock institutions of Canada's constitution and political system are currently. At its core, since 1982, are three familiar pillars: Cabinet–parliamentary government; federalism, centred on a division of legislative powers but also on important fiscal principles; and the Charter of Rights and Freedoms, which defines both individual and group rights. But fourth and fifth pillars are also present now – namely, the quasi-constitutional international free-trade deals and the AIT. We cannot quite accurately refer to them as full constitutional pillars because both lack the full legal apparatus that normally attaches to constitutional provisions. But pillars they are, in the sense that they have a solidity of presence in the minds and strategies of governmental policy makers. All policy must now be designed with an eye to whether all of the rules of the game are being adhered to, and these rules now include those of the international-trade and internal-trade quasi-constitutional realms.

If this is what free-trade federalism means in some broad sense, it must also be seen in terms of the many subtleties that have been shown to arise in the negotiation of the fifth pillar. Indeed, many will object to referring to it as a pillar at all because they are critical of the AIT as being neither a constitutional provision nor a good trade agreement on the international model. Initial assessments of the AIT have come from three sources: business; scholars from the law and economics disciplines, and, more slowly emerging, scholars specializing in federal–provincial relations.

The most explicit business commentary has come from the Canadian Chamber of Commerce. The chamber is 'highly critical of the fundamental weaknesses, flaws and loopholes' in the agreement (Canadian Chamber of Commerce 1996, 1). It calls for a reduction in exceptions, an enforceable dispute-resolution process, and effective private action. It uses not only normal economic arguments, but also the national-unity issue. It concludes that 'weak internal trade links mean less reason to stay united' (Canadian Chamber of Commerce 1996, 21). It also calls for direct business involvement in future negotiations. Similar criticisms are made by other business-oriented analysts (Parsons and Arcus 1996).

The assessment produced by scholars of law and economics is best reflected in several C.D. Howe Institute publications. These assessments tend to start with a view that the AIT is a needed first step, but then express a wide range of criticisms about the contradictions in the agreement, its weak dispute-resolution mechanisms, and, even by 1995, its slipping deadlines for implementing some provisions (Trebilcock and Schwanen 1995). Individual legal scholars such as Robert Howse are also critical of the agreement but exhibit a greater edge of optimism by suggesting concretely how they think the federal government can build on the agreement through the use of its constitutional powers (Howse 1995, 8–14).

Mainstream scholars of federalism have been slower to comment, perhaps because they are less inclined to want to see federalism in trade-oriented terms. For example, Donald Lenihan focuses on the 'legitimate objectives' features of the agreement and, though aware of the contradictions in the AIT, he is much more tolerant of them as a needed democratic and governing compromise (Lenihan 1995). This is certainly also the view of left-of-centre criticisms such as that emerging from the Canadian Centre for Policy Alternatives (Sinclair 1994). The federalism literature focuses on the shift of powers to the federal government and to the downward pressure the AIT may put on standards.

One of the difficulties with these initial assessments is that they focus on the agreement without undertaking a complementary analysis of the politics of the negotiations themselves or attempting to situate them in the context of larger political forces or perspectives. This book has taken these forces more explicitly into account. Indeed, the negotiations themselves, coupled with the larger pressures from free-trade values and interests, are what cause us to argue that the AIT warrants being designated a fifth pillar in the overall Canadian institutional lexicon.

When seen in this light, free-trade federalism is a very large and complex subject. We have examined only aspects of this large terrain through a focus on the AIT and the way it was negotiated. Negotiations are always a complex interplay of interests, ideas, issues, structures, timing, and personalities. As stressed from the outset, this account of the negotiations, while we hope a useful beginning, cannot be considered to be a complete one. We do not pay full attention to the interpersonal dynamics, nor do we cover all the sectors negotiated.

The previous eight chapters have, however, supplied some of the necessary basic pieces of the analytical picture: first, a sense of the issues involved and the basic content and architecture of the agreement; second, a framework that showed the evolution of three key policy fields and a review of how internal trade got on the agenda and what the negotiating institutions looked like; third, an account of the macro negotiating dynamics and issues; fourth, an analysis of three sets of sectoral negotiations, embracing eight different negotiating tables; and, finally, dispute-resolution debates and outcomes.

Before offering overall conclusions on the processes and institutions involved and the prospects for their future adaptation as central features of free-trade federalism, it is useful to summarize briefly the basic findings of the eight-chapter journey.

Analytical Summary: The AIT Process in General

First, we conclude that the Agreement on Internal Trade is an extremely important development in Canadian federal–provincial relations largely because, despite its weaknesses, it genuinely advances the cause of internal trade, but also because it does indeed remove or lessen the capacities of governments, especially provincial governments, to act in ways that had been possible in the previous three decades. It also represents a considerable penetration into domestic agendas and institution-building of the globalization-led liberalized international-trade agenda. This is reflected in the very architecture of the agreement, its language and terminology, and the key influence of the trade policy community.

The negotiations on the agreement represent one of the first occasions where a macro multi–policy field approach to federal–provincial relations was used. More will be said on this point below. The multi–policy field negotiating approach was the dominant logic and driver of the process, but it also encountered within the various sectors different continuing instances of bilateral and multilateral federalism, and thus federalism's normal decision making also functioned.

It is also crucial to conclude on an overall basis that, in effect, what the provinces were required to do under the AIT was exactly what the federal government had to do during the FTA, NAFTA, and GATT negotiations – determine what governing capacities it would give up, lessen, or discipline itself in using, in the name of promoting liberalized trade and, it was hoped, a more dynamic and competitive Canadian economy.

Chapter 2 provided a broader historical framework and context for this overall development. It traced the basic trajectories of regional-industrial policy, trade policy, and federal–provincial policy, and provided an initial sense of the related policy communities. While each field is complex, the broad pattern of change in the confluence of these fields is quite clear. Trade policy was ascending aggressively and crossing borders into the realm of domestic governance, including areas of provincial jurisdiction. Regional-industrial policy was on the defensive and in decline as the global and national micro economy changed, as government budgets shrank, and as trade rules themselves made old-style regional-industrial policy less and less possible. Federal–provincial policy in its broadest sense was also on the defensive in that the Charlottetown and Meech failures were fresh in mind. Federal–provincial policy formation had experienced a variety of modes of decision making but nothing that approached the style that the AIT was about to involve. A multi–policy field negotiation-centred form of policy making was a new innovation. Chapter 2 also showed that the debate about the social union was not a key impetus for the AIT, although it was raised in the negotiation as a counterplay to the logic of the economic union by several provinces. Further comments on the social union are offered below.

We have seen in chapter 3 that the internal-trade negotiations had a difficult gestation period in that, from the mid-1980s until about 1990, the issue of internal trade was simply not high on the priority list. It had some important roots in the constitutional discussions in the early 1980s and was a factor in the Canada Round in the early 1990s. The early views of academics and the Macdonald Commission were a further impetus, but internal trade was not a political priority until further paradigm shifts in thinking and learning occurred, in part through pressure from big business. Initially, this involved the listing of the problem in a larger nexus of regional-development issues, and then received greater attention as crucial new international-trade agreements were negotiated in the late 1980s and early 1990s.

The prospect of the 1993 election forced a useful hiatus and enabled some important preparatory work to be done, in some cases to allow research to be completed and the system of negotiating tables to be worked out, and, in an overall sense, to allow the basic architecture of the agreement to be thought through. The drafting of some kind of initial text also was crucial in the negotiations that then truly began in the first six months of 1994.

The core of the internal-trade agreement was the battle over general rules versus exceptions and legitimate objectives. In short, it centred on two competing visions among the participating governments: those who saw it primarily as a trade agreement and those who tended to see it more as an agreement on governance in a federation. The political fault lines accordingly centred also on dispute-resolution provisions and the role of regional policy and Crown corporations. Procurement and investment issues also loomed large in the end-game. The final pact was the product of a negotiating and political (including personal) interplay among the federal government, a neutral chair and secretariat, and twelve provincial and territorial governments. As in any complex multi-party negotiation over a twelve-month period, the nature of the interplay had both permanent or stable alliances and shifting ones. We have by no means been able to capture all the subtleties of the process, but some broad patterns are evident from the analysis in chapter 4.

The federal government, the secretariat, Alberta, and Manitoba were the most supportive of an agreement that maximized the general rules and effective dispute-settlement provisions and minimized the exceptions. They were the most inclined to see AIT as a trade agreement. Quebec was also supportive, and indeed the presence of both Alberta and Quebec as allies of the federal government was an interesting reversal of many of the normal recent configurations of federal–provincial politics where they were often the most truculent about federal intentions. Chapter 4 showed that the three provincial NDP governments did not agree on every matter, but they were united strategically and philosophically, by a scepticism about a free-trade agenda in general and about federal government intentions. They also supported the need to preserve crucial powers of government. Ontario, B.C., and Saskatchewan led the forces that would have preferred a sectoral approach but that, failing that in a resulting agreement, sought to maximize the exceptions and legitimate objectives and minimize general rules and dispute settlement.

Quebec was supportive of an internal-trade agreement, but its negotiating approach was inevitably couched in terms of an expected late 1994 election. It had to show support for an economic union without giving up, or appearing to give up, provincial powers. The fact of this election, and of the possibility of a Parti Québécois separatist victory, was the unstated bottom line for those provinces which otherwise might be tempted to walk away from the negotiations. Had they done so, federalism would have visibly failed for the third time in four years on a major negotiation.

The remaining players, the Atlantic provinces, and the two territorial governments, signed the agreement and in varying ways supported a more open internal market. But they also sensed that they were operating from a position of recognized political weakness in a negotiating sense. Nova Scotia in particular saw the internal-trade agreement less as an opportunity and more as an exercise in damage control, where defensive postures were the only real option. New Brunswick was selectively more aggressive in its pursuit of open markets, in part because it had resigned itself that the older options of relying on federal regional policy incentives were over. All of the smaller provinces still wanted room to practise various kinds of regional policy within their own boundaries.

Our sample of key sets of sectoral negotiations show at least three overall types of sectoral subjects and arenas of negotiating. Procurement and regional development were largely handled by the main table. They also had major ministerial involvement, thus testifying to the central place these issues occupied politically and economically. It is fair to say that the

AIT opens up more procurement to pan-Canadian bidding but also that a lot of the legwork for this had been done by the previously signed regional procurement agreements.

It is also reasonable to conclude that the general use of policies governing regional economic development has been disciplined to a greater extent than before. The disciplining comes partly from events outside the AIT – namely, the reduction of fiscal capacity by most governments. But it also comes from the AIT provisions for defining regional-development framework policies with transparent criteria and some reporting requirements.

At the same time, the larger importance of regional economic-development, and vagueness as to how to assess general economic development policies, as distinct from explicit regional policies, remain. These issues and dynamics are still engrained in the very nature of governing in a federation and in a pan-continental Canada, where economic regions are simply too diverse for only trade-driven rules to prevail. These issues had to be accommodated in the AIT just as they had been in the procurement/national/regional aspects of the FTA, NAFTA, and WTO international agreements.

Our second cluster of sectoral areas – investment, labour mobility, and environmental protection – were all seen as horizontal aspects that cut across all of the vertical sectors of the economy. None of these horizontal framework areas succeeded in becoming a horizontal chapter that took total precedence over other chapters in the AIT. They do, however, all have *some* aspects of supremacy over other chapters. This was the natural outgrowth of the inner tension in the negotiations between those who saw the agreement as first and foremost a trade negotiation and those who saw it as primarily a negotiation in which other values about governance and legitimate objectives should either prevail or occupy appropriate policy and political space in the Canadian federation.

The analysis has shown that in two of the three areas – investment and labour mobility – the federal government was undoubtedly the demandeur arguing for a principles and rules-based approach versus a 'listing and solving' of barriers approach, as preferred by most provinces. Once again, the federal government found allies for its views, mainly Alberta and Manitoba, but also considerable opposition, headed by Ontario, B.C., and Saskatchewan. The sectoral tables also reveal many more subtle, particular positions from various provinces, as would be expected in complex sectoral situations.

The third set of sectoral negotiations perhaps revealed these provincial particularities even more starkly. The natural-resource sectors of agricultural and food goods, resource processing, and energy dealt not only with real vertical sectors, but also with areas where provincial ownership of the resource was extremely important. Each sectoral table sought in its own way to advance internal trade but always in the context of quite deep-seated concerns about provincial control of most natural resources.

The agricultural and food goods table achieved advances in the realm of technical standards, but only by ensuring that the larger barriers found in supply management and transportation were not dealt with in internal-trade political fora. The table dealing with the processing of natural resources struggled over where to draw the line regarding products that were close to the primary resource and those that were farther up the value-added production chain. Progress was made in reducing barriers, but, once again there were enormous sensitivities regarding the provinces' powers over resource ownership and control. The resource-processing negotiating group also spent a considerable part of their negotiating efforts fending off the feared incursions of the environmental table.

The energy table ultimately failed to produce an energy chapter because of sensitivities regarding the wheeling of electrical energy. But it was also weighed down by the considerable problems felt by many provinces regarding not only how to manage intraprovincial electricity trade, but also how to deal with the very real political power and prestige of provincially owned utilities.

Institutions and Multi–Policy Field Negotiations

The conclusions that can be offered on institutions and on multi–policy field negotiations as a policy process are varied. Some can be seen to flow from the analysis, while others arise more from the authors' judgment about the likely balances arising from future developments. In commenting, we must also distinguish between institutions that were involved *in* the negotiations and those *established* by the agreement itself.

In an overall sense, the mix of institutions adopted for the negotiations can be considered to have been reasonably successful simply because it did produce an agreement that goes beyond some minor amendment to federalism. The multilayered players of the CMIT, chief negotiators, neutral chair and secretariat, and sectoral tables with shared-out chairs was necessary to success both in managerial and in political terms. In many respects, this structure borrowed from international-trade negotiation machinery. The possible exception is the role of the neutral chair. This player was quite crucial not only because federal–provincial and interprovincial tensions were still quite raw following the Meech Lake and Charlottetown constitutional defeats, but also because the federal government was not, and could not be, neutral in the negotiations. It had an agenda and, indeed, was the main demandeur. The role of Arthur Mauro was therefore extremely important. It would be hard to envisage future internal-trade rounds that would not require someone with the kind of mixed senior political and problem-solving and mediating skills Arthur Mauro supplied in the 1993–4 process.

The role of a secretariat prior to and during the process of negotiations is also of considerable import. In the latter 1980s, it was probably only the presence of a secretariat that helped keep the internal-trade issues alive as a kind of 'voice from within.' In the actual negotiations, the secretariat (with its provincial counterparts) obviously supplied not only the necessary paper flow, but also certain kinds of mediation activity and research. One of the more problematical aspects of secretariat-style roles in such negotiations is whether certain kinds of research or 'received knowledge' are adequate to the task or even wanted by the various players.

For example, there were differences from the outset as to whether players agreed with, or had seriously critiqued, the central issue of whether the dynamic losses to the Canadian economy caused by internal-trade barriers were big, medium, or small. All three of the sectoral areas examined in chapter 6 included aspects on which the parties agreed they had very little information, such as which environmental measures had trade impacts, and whether labour-mobility barriers were big, medium, or simply irritating. It was, in brief, difficult to know how much was based on anecdotes and lists of grievances as distinct from other kinds of evidence.

The various work plans and reporting requirements in the agreement are likely to produce better information for the next round of negotiations, but this is in itself no guarantee that this information will be analysed and made usable for any subsequent round of negotiations. No multiple-field dynamic trade or trade–federal/provincial negotiation can ever be 'objectivity incarnate.' Negotiations are also about power and juggernauts with agendas, but ultimately a reasonable balance of objective knowledge must be assembled. Let it simply be said that the 1994 negotiations were far from perfect in this regard.

What can be said in conclusion about the interplay among the three overall policy communities referred to in chapter 2 – namely, regional-

industrial policy, trade policy, and federal–provincial policy? In the negotiations as a whole, trade policy was on the offensive, and both regional-
industrial policy and federal–provincial policy were on the defensive.
However, within this overall trend there are clearly some sectoral varia-
tions and subtleties.

The inward tentacles of NAFTA and GATT and their attendant liberal
trade ideas were evident in the sectoral tables, especially in the investment regimes being advocated, and in some respects in the environmental protection chapter. The labour mobility chapter had fewer immediate
international-trade links *per se*, although the example of the European
Union had relevance in the debate regarding the preferred approach of
mutual recognition of occupational qualifications as opposed to full harmonized standards. The labour mobility table was also without doubt the
table that had the least experience with trade-like negotiations since this
area had been entirely a domestic federal–provincial field.

These inter–policy field and –policy community patterns were of
course criss-crossed with other institutional realities in the negotiations.
For example, the degree to which each sectoral table was tied to the central politics of the chief negotiators' table varied and was therefore important. Each table, of course, had some connection as the deal was
hammered out, but the investment table in particular was bound up,
especially because of the links with procurement and regional-development policies. The labour mobility, environmental protection, agricultural and food goods, and resource processing tables had somewhat
greater independence, in part because they were functioning within, and
being negotiated by, quite well-established federal–provincial policy communities and institutions.

As we saw in chapter 6, there was also a sense in some tables that strategies and negotiating relationships were different. The environment table
was not primarily a federal-versus-provincial battle; rather, it involved a
process whereby the environmental negotiators saw themselves in common cause against the trade community, and hence sought to preserve
recent NAFTA gains regarding the recognition of sustainable development without being swamped by a trade-oriented negotiating juggernaut.
The labour mobility table was also tactically limited in that in many
respects this was the first full-scale negotiation on labour mobility, especially regarding the professions, and hence there was a sense of making
progress simply by getting key issues recognized.

The 1994 negotiation process was also, in one sense, unlike recent
trade-agreement processes and unlike recent federal–provincial relations

in that there was a decided absence of public and interest-group involvement. Indeed, in terms of federal–provincial relations, the decision process was a throwback to 'executive federalism.' The behind-the-scenes route was perhaps chosen for sensible reasons. After all, the Charlottetown constitutional processes involved public fora, which ranged from legislative bodies to referenda, and they failed. International-trade negotiations can also be quite elite-based, but they typically have involved private-sector processes through the sectoral advisory groups (the SAGITs) and other vehicles.

The analysis shows that interest groups were not systematically involved in the AIT, but that some forms of consultation occurred, albeit within the tight time periods involved. The national business lobby clearly helped get the issue on the agenda and kept up pressure during the negotiations, mainly through its links with the federal government and Industry Canada. Alberta also had a form of consultation with its business community. It is important to note, however, that this muted input from interest groups was not the result of their restriction by negotiators, who in fact would have welcomed more contact, especially during the information-gathering stages of the negotiations. The lack of interest-group involvement appears to be the result of a more pervasive lack of general interest. It remains to be seen whether this pattern continues during future negotiations.

The sectoral tables also varied in the extent to which they involved outside interest groups. In the case of the environmental protection chapter, the contact with ENGOs was remarkably small, especially given the normally tenacious vigilance of the ENGOs. Some consultation did occur, however. It was in the labour-mobility-chapter negotiations that consultation with interests was most in evidence. This was undoubtedly because the regulation of professions was central. This consultation was federally led and involved national associations rather than the undoubtedly more influential provincial professions and self-regulating bodies.

Dispute Resolution, the Trade-and-Commerce Power, and 'Rules about Rules'

A final aspect of AIT institutions and of its central political aspects is dispute resolution, the debate about the trade-and-commerce power, and the extent to which the AIT contains 'rules about rules' regarding standards and the regulatory activities of government. Chapter 8 showed how the negotiations on dispute resolution and institutions, and the final content of these provisions, reflected the shadowy grey zone in which the participants sought to place the agreement.

The AIT is de facto a side deal to the constitution, but it was not supposed to change the constitution. It was a political agreement that was intended to avoid the courts, but it was also to be complied with in an authoritative and effective manner. In much the same way that many regulations and guidelines in government are seen to be the outcomes of 'negotiating in the shadow of the law,' the Agreement on Internal Trade and its dispute-resolution provisions are the product of negotiating in the shadow of the constitution. Again, this is why some commentators would be disinclined to refer to the AIT as a new pillar of Canadian governance.

The dual dispute-resolution avenues – government-to-government and person-to-government – were designed by governments and for the convenience of governments. Though the dispute-resolution procedures are said to be based on a spirit of cooperation, it is equally possible to say that their elongated nature is based on the fact that the governments did not fully trust each other, and trusted private interests and interest groups even less.

We have seen, however, that these complex processes are also due to the nature of the negotiations themselves and to the architecture of the agreement. Above all it was the matrix architecture of the agreement itself which forced the first stages of dispute resolution into the chapter or sectoral realm.

These complex features are also why assessments vary about whether the agreement and the dispute-resolution features enhance or detract from the federal government's exercise of its trade-and-commerce powers and hence its lead role in the enhancement of the Canadian economic union. Those who think that it has constrained the trade-and-commerce power fear that it has set limits around the powers, and that the courts, using doctrines of 'constitutional convention,' may simply conclude that what is practised (namely, the internal agreement as a living document) is what the constitutional trade-and-commerce power in fact is. Since the trade-and-commerce power has never been fully defined, the agreement is what will define it.

The alternative line of argument, which this study supports, is that federal trade-and-commerce powers are in fact enhanced by the agreement because it is the discriminatory power of provincial governments that have been most reined in. In short, the range of available provincial policy instruments has been narrowed. Many actions that provinces previously did take are simply less and less possible.

A similar constraining effect has been created by the way in which the agreement deals with standards and regulatory measures. Thus we have seen that the federal government and key supportive provinces sought to enshrine international trade–derived principles and concepts, including mutual recognition, harmonization, performance-based regulation, and science-based regulation. The final AIT shows that, though progress was made in this overall direction, there was by no means full agreement on 'rules about rules,' and indeed that several provinces resisted these concepts when cast in a domestic context and when advocated by a federal government whose overall agenda many provinces disagreed with.

Future Free-Trade Federalism: The AIT, Quebec, and the Social Union

A further cluster of conclusions or observations about the future of Canadian free-trade federalism can be drawn. These centre around three issues or pressures: the next steps in improving the AIT; the Quebec sovereignty issue; and the articulation of concerns about a social union as the other side of the coin of free-trade federalism.

With regard to the further development of the AIT, there are inevitably a mixture of process and substantive issues involved. Perhaps, the first point to note is the simple issue of whether there can be or should be new 'rounds' of negotiations, as opposed to more limited processes for improving the AIT.

A formal second round is certainly a possibility. The various work programs and reporting requirements suggest that many items must be revisited. Ontario and other reluctant provinces did concur that any agreement should be organic and therefore would be built upon and improved. If the international-trade analogy is continued, then one of course has the example of the GATT, where the original agreement in 1947 was followed by the Kennedy Round, the Tokyo Round, and the recent Uruguay Round. The internal-trade-agreement process could therefore now be looking for its 'Kennedy' Round.

The concept of rounds, or indeed the inherent notion of there being a multi–policy field, multi-party negotiation, involves the question of how big or how broad such a round should be. If it is too narrow or confined to a small set of sectors, then it is more difficult to achieve trade-offs, in part because interests can mobilize against the few more than they can against many sectors. At the international free-trade level this had been borne out repeatedly wherever sectoral free-trade approaches had been advocated (such as in the early 1980s between Canada and the United

States). However, for the next internal-trade round, the question is 'How big is big enough?' for a round to overcome these problems.

Getting a muscular political deadline for negotiations is also crucially involved in such questions. As emphasized, without a firm deadline negotiations cease to be negotiations and simply become endless incrementalized policy making (which, of course, many players and interests might prefer).

The federal government is still the main demandeur in this process, and thus it will push for as wide-ranging a set of issues as possible. Many provinces are unwilling to enter a negotiation that is anywhere near as broad as the first. Indeed, some would prefer no further negotiations at all. And yet they agreed to many areas where work plans were launched.

If and when a new internal-trade negotiating step or round occurs, there certainly are many areas/chapters that could be on the agenda. Some of these will also be propelled by obligations and pressures from the international-trade realm, especially keeping in mind that 'trade' in the international realm is increasingly and mainly about domestic-policy measures rather than about border measures. Thus the next steps could certainly deal with labour mobility, energy, agricultural and food goods, environmental protection, investment, and regional matters. Federal policies and exemptions from the AIT will also be looked at more closely.[1]

Dispute resolution is bound to become a key area again, but if the negotiations are held right away, experience with the new processes will still be very limited and there will be very few cases of dispute resolution. The federal government and Alberta will again press for stronger dispute-resolution provisions, but the political issues around this are still quite complex, and even unpredictable. For example, in the 1993–4 round, it is clear that dispute settlement with private-action provisions was generally seen as a device through which businesses could take action against governments erecting barriers, with the emphasis on the 'barriers.' But the dispute-resolution provisions apply to the whole agreement, so it is possible in another round that other social interests will see the dispute-

---

1 As this book went to press, further negotiating progress had occurred on a chapter-by-chapter basis rather than through a full new round. In February 1998, agreement was reached on covering procurement by the MASH sector. Only British Columbia did not sign on to the MASH agreement. An energy chapter was also ready for signing, largely because the key problems of the electricity sector had been overcome. In addition, there had been progress in reducing the list of entities (mainly Crown corporations) excluded from the procurement chapter. Impetus for further progress had come at both the Premiers' Conference in August 1997 and an Internal Trade Ministers' meeting in February 1998.

settlement provisions as needing strengthening to ensure that other provisions also enjoy full compliance, such as legitimate objectives, environmental standards, and various exemptions.

Some of the pressures in the next round, on dispute settlement and on other areas, thus depend upon whether it is designed again as executive federalism in operation or whether broader interest-group and public input is invited as a systematic part of the process at either the national or the provincial level. It is doubtful that, in the next steps, interests will not be aware that internal trade is about much more that technical matters of trade.

The more that the internal-trade agreement is seen to be both an extension into Canada of international-trade rules *and* a crucial side deal on the constitution, the more likely it is that broader public input will be pushed for. These pressures may also alter the evolving balance regarding the degree to which the AIT can be seen to be a political agreement as distinct from a legal agreement. The desire to keep the agreement or dispute resolution out of the courts may follow the path that has partially transpired in areas such as environmental assessment. Federal approaches which were thought to be confineable to the status of *being* guidelines were challenged in the courts and ruled to be law-like. It is hard not to see some provisions of the Agreement on Internal Trade moving out of the shadows of a political agreement and into a legal, or quasi-legal or even quasi-constitutional, realm.

A final feature of the next steps is that there are likely to be newer provincial demands for greater involvement in international-trade processes than they have had in the past. This could involve pressures/demands to strengthen Clause 1809.4. The dynamic here is a simple one. If internal-trade agreements essentially move more and more into areas of provincial jurisdiction, then the provinces will want a stake in federal trade-policy making. In short, if trade is everything, then everyone wants a say in trade policy, external and internal.

The notion of a further AIT round assumes, of course, a fairly normally functioning Canadian federation. But the dynamics of the Quebec sovereigntist option and how it is resolved are also a part of future free-trade federalism. The political situation in Quebec, with a sovereigntist Parti Québécois (PC) government in power and another referendum to be held, will loom large. As we have seen, in the early 1990s, both the Parti Québécois and the Quebec Liberal party advocated versions of a European Union model for Canada–Quebec relations. The Quebec Government of Lucien Bouchard will approach the next referendum knowing that it will have to show that it can make an internal market work because the political saleability of the sovereigntist argument to many 'soft nationalist' Quebec voters is based in part on a promise that they will not lose their access to the Canadian economic union or the continental markets via the FTA and NAFTA. But such a promise involves the commitments of other partners in the Canadian federation, and it is also dependent on the new state of federal politics, where the Western Canada–centred Reform Party holds the reins as Official Opposition in Parliament.

But a sovereigntist state, if that is what materializes, also has strong instincts to want to preserve governing powers and capacities because, after all, that is what a sovereigntist state is all about. Quebec's past preferences for a 'Quebec Inc.' form of interventionist industrial policy may be on the wane in a deficit-fighting Bouchard Quebec government, but it would be hard for any sovereigntist Quebec government to resist the use of at least some of the industrial-policy tools left in the micro economic-policy tool kit. Thus the conundrum is real. If the Quebec government is going to use such powers, then it cannot adhere to the AIT deal it says it supports and that it is promising voters to maintain in a sovereigntist future. But if it does not use its interventionist powers, the further logical question is: what then is it seeking to be sovereign about? Clearly, there are other features of governing around which a sovereigntist argument can be built, but these are then more significantly centred on social policy and the social union.

This brings us full circle to what many interests in Canada, both during and after the AIT process, and both during and after the FTA and NAFTA, regard as the missing social dimension. As we have stressed, even the coining of the phrase 'social union' or of concepts such as 'social cohesion' is itself a counterplay to the language of the economic union. We have not focused on the social union, but it is possible to conclude that it will undoubtedly figure much more prominently in the next overall phase of free-trade federalism. Several factors suggest that this counterplay is already necessarily under way.

First, the second Chrétien government, with its deficit under better control, but facing the PQ in Quebec and the Reform Party in Western Canada, has begun to think more concretely about what kinds of policies might in fact constitute policies of social cohesion beyond 2000 (Policy Research Committee 1996). Some of this focus on social cohesion is undoubtedly a new form of political sloganeering, but there are also genuine concerns at the centre of such initiatives that are felt in a larger G-7 context and are also a response to the global free-trade era. Second, as suggested above, it is likely that, in new AIT or other policy arenas, broader interest-groups, including social-union activists, will insist on being involved in way that they were not in AIT Round I. Third, even in the narrower terrain of an AIT 'Round II' that looked much like the 1994 round, there are already latent concerns about job-creation, labour-mobility, environmental, and other standard-setting issues.

However, if the social union is the other half of free-trade federalism, it will clearly still be reacting to the agenda of the first half of free-trade federalism. After all, the economic union that was at the centre of the political impetus for the AIT was itself centred in part on a social view that said that Canadians should have as individuals the freedom to take part in the Canadian economy in all parts of a unity-enhancing Canadian economic union. A broader view of a social union will undoubtedly also be needed to preserve Canada in a new century, but it is clear that the underpinnings and conceptions of the economic union have now been permanently changed.

Given recent democratic trends, the 1994 process was indeed remarkably contained, and hence the question arises as to whether future rounds of negotiations will be allowed to be so contained. This is the case especially because there are genuine and quite broad democratic concerns about the precise balances to be struck among the fundamental values involved as revealed in the debates and stances within the 1994 negotiations. In short, how much of the agenda should be determined by trade ideas and rationales? What basic aspects of governance in a federation need to be preserved and defended? What visions of national unity and social cohesion ought to prevail or be accommodated: a country of mobile citizens, workers, and investors with entrenched rights anywhere in the country and/or a country of provinces with quasi-sovereign provinces sharing jurisdictions and real governing capacities with a national government committed to changed definitions of social well-being?

References

Abele, Frances, ed. 1991. *How Ottawa spends, 1991–92: The politics of fragmentation.* Ottawa: Carleton University Press.

Abelson, Donald E., and Michael Lusztig. 1996 The consistency of inconsistency: Tracing Ontario's opposition to the North American Free Trade Agreement. *Canadian Journal of Political Science* 29 (December): 681–98.

Agriculture and Agri-Food Canada. 1995. *Securing our future in agriculture and agri-food.* Ottawa: Agriculture and Agri-Food Canada.

Albert, Michel. 1993. *Capitalism against capitalism.* London: Whurr.

Anderson, F.J. 1985. *Natural Resources in Canada.* Toronto: Methuen.

Appleton, Barry. 1994. *Navigating NAFTA.* Toronto: Carswell.

Archer, K., R. Gibbins, R. Knopff, and Leslie Pal. 1995. *Parameters of power: Canada's political institutions.* Toronto: Nelson.

Atkinson, Michael. 1993. *Governing Canada: Institutions and public policy.* Toronto: Harcourt Brace Jovanovich.

Axelrod, R. 1984. *The evolution of cooperation.* New York: Basic Books.

Bach, S., and S.D. Phillips. 1997. Constructing a new social union: Child care beyond infancy? In *How Ottawa spends, 1996–97: Seeing red,* ed. Gene Swimmer, 235–58. Ottawa: Carleton University Press.

Bakan, J. 1992. 'What's wrong with social rights?' In J. Bakan and D. Schneiderman, *Social justice and the constitution: Perspectives on a social union for Canada.* 85–99. Ottawa: Carleton University Press.

Bakan, J., and D. Schneiderman. 1992. 'Introduction.' In *Social justice and the constitution: Perspectives on a social union for Canada,* 1–16. Ottawa: Carleton University Press.

Banting, Keith G. 1988. Federalism, social reform and the spending power. *Canadian Public Policy* 14: 581–92.

– 1996. Social policy. In *Border crossings: The internationlization of Canadian public policy*, ed. Bruce Doern, Les Pal, and Brian Tomlin, 27–54. Toronto: Oxford University Press.

Bayefsky, A.F. 1989. *Canada's Constitution Act of 1982 and Amendments: A documentary history*. Toronto: McGraw-Hill Ryerson.

Bayes, Michael D. 1986. Professional power and self-regulation. *Business and Professional Ethics Journal* 5/2: 26–46.

Bence, Jean-François, and Murray Smith. 1989. Subsidies and trade laws: The Canada–US dimension. *International Economic Issues*, April–May: 1–36.

Benedickson, Jamie, G. Bruce Doern, and Nancy Olewiler. 1994. *Getting the green light: Environmental regulation and investment in Canada*. Toronto: C.D. Howe Institute.

Best, Michael H. 1990. *The new competition: Institutions of industrial restructuring*. Cambridge: Polity.

Blais, Andre. 1985. The debate on Canadian industrial policy. In *Industrial Policy*, ed. Andre Blais, 55–82. Toronto: University of Toronto Press.

Boadway, R.W. 1995. Fiscal federalism and social policy reform. *Canadian Journal of Regional Science* 18: 199–220.

Boardman, Robert. 1992. The multilateral dimension: Canada in the international system. In *Canadian environmental policy: Ecosystems, politics and processes*, ed. R. Boardman, 224–45. Toronto: Oxford University Press.

Boddez, Thomas, and Michael Trebilcock. 1993. *Unfinished business: Reforming trade remedy laws in North America*. Toronto: C.D. Howe Institute.

Brams, S.J. 1985. *Superpower games: Applying game theory to superpower conflict*. New Haven: Yale University Press.

Brams, S.J., D.M. Kilgour, and S. Merrill. 1991. Arbitration procedures. In *Negotiation analysis*, ed. H.P. Young. Ann Arbor: University of Michigan Press.

Brander, J.A. 1985. Economic policy formation in a federal State: A game theoretic approach. In *Intergovernmental relations*, ed. R. Simeon, Toronto: University of Toronto Press.

Breton, A. 1989. The theory of competitive federalism. In *Federalism in Canada: Selected Readings*, ed. G. Stevenson, 457–502. Toronto: McClelland & Stewart.

Brock, K.L. 1991. The politics of process. In *Canada: The state of the federation, 1991*, ed. D.M. Brown, Kingston: Institute of Intergovernmental Relations.

Brown, David, F. Lazar, and Daniel Schwanen. 1992. *Free to move: Strengthening the Canadian economic union*. Toronto: C.D. Howe Institute.

Brown, D.M. 1989. Canadian federalism and trade policy: The Uruguay Round agenda. In *Canada: The state of the federation, 1989*, ed. R.L. Watts and D.M. Brown, 211–35. Kingston: Institute of Intergovernmental Relations.

Brown, D.M., and R. Young, eds. 1992. *Canada: The state of the federation, 1992*. Kingston: Institute of Intergovernmental Affairs.

Brown, D.M., and J.W. Rose, eds. 1995. *Canada: The state of the federation, 1995.* Kingston: Institute of Intergovernmental Affairs.

Cairns, A. 1977. The governments and societies of Canadian federalism. *Canadian Journal of Political Science* 10/4: 695–725.

Campbell, R.M., and L.A. Pal. 1991. *The real worlds of Canadian politics: Cases in process and policy,* 2d ed. Peterborough, ON: Broadview Press.

Canada. 1940. *Report of the Royal Commission on Dominion-Provincial Relations.* Rowell-Sirois Commission. Ottawa: King's Printer.

– 1985. *Intergovernmental position paper: On the principles and framework for regional economic development.* Ottawa: Minister of Supply and Services.

– 1985b. *Report of the Royal Commission on the Economic Union and Development Prospects for Canada,* Volume 3. Ottawa: Minister of Supply and Services.

– 1988. *Energy and Canadians into the 21st century.* Ottawa: Minister of Supply and Services.

– 1994. *Agreement on Internal Trade.* Ottawa: Government of Canada

Canada West Foundation. 1996, April. *Selling it to the world: A profile of Western Canadian merchandise exports.* Calgary: Canada West Foundation.

Canadian Chamber of Commerce. 1996. *The Agreement on Internal Trade and Interprovincial Trade Flows: Building a strong united Canada.* Toronto: Canadian Chamber of Commerce.

Canadian Chamber of Commerce and La Chambre de Commerce du Québec. 1995, May. Interprovincial trade: Engine of economic growth. Montreal.

Canadian Council of Ministers of the Environment. 1996, 31 May. Environment ministers embrace new vision for CCME. Press Release, Ottawa.

Carty, R.T., ed. 1996. *Politics, policy and government in British Columbia.* Vancouver: UBC Press.

Chandler, Marsha, and William M. Chandler, eds. 1979. *Public policy and provincial politics.* Toronto: McGraw-Hill Ryerson.

Chrétien, Prime Minister Jean. 1994, 18 July. 'Statement on the Internal Trade Agreement.' Ottawa.

Cohen, A. 1990. *A deal undone: The making and breaking of the Meech Lake Accord.* Vancouver: Douglas & McIntyre.

Cohen, David. 1995. The Internal Trade Agreement: Furthering the Canadian economic disunion? *Canadian Business Law Journal* 25/2 (July): 257–79.

Coleman, W.D., and Grace Skogstad, eds. 1990. *Policy communities and public policy in Canada.* Toronto: Copp Clark Pitman.

Committee of Ministers on Internal Trade. 1992, 4 December. 'Internal Trade ministers propose an accelerated and comprehensive negotiations process for the removal of barriers.' News release.

– 1993, 18 March. 'Governments agree on comprehensive negotiations to reduce internal trade barriers.' News release.

- 1994, 10 January. 'CMIT: Directions to chief negotiator.'
- 1994, 20 January. 'Progress on internal trade negotiations.' News release.
- 1994, 7 April. 'Ministers provide further directions to chief negotiators for internal trade.' News release.
- 1994, 28 June. 'Internal trade negotiations: Agreement-in-principle.' News release.

Cook, Curtis, ed. 1994. *Constitutional predicament.* Montreal: McGill-Queen's University Press.

Copeland, Brian. 1993. Interprovincial barriers to trade: A Review of the empirical evidence from a British Columbia perspective.' Paper prepared for the British Columbia Ministry of Economic Development, Small Business and Trade. Victoria.

Courchene, T.J. 1987. *Social policy in the 1990s: Agenda for reform.* Toronto: C.D. Howe Institute.
- 1991. *In praise of renewed federalism.* Toronto: C.D. Howe Institute.
- 1992, 6 June. Mons pays, c'est l'hiver: Reflections of a market populist. Presidential address to the Canadian Economics Association, Charlottetown, PEI.
- 1995. *Celebrating flexibility: An interpretative essay on the evolution of Canadian federalism.* Toronto: C.D. Howe Institute.

Courchene, T.J., and Arthur E. Stewart, eds. 1992. *Quebec Inc II: Financing innovation.* Kingston: Queen's University School of Policy Studies.

Daniels, R.J., ed. 1996. *Ontario Hydro at the millennium.* Montreal: McGill-Queen's University Press.

de la Mothe, John, and Gilles Paquet, eds. 1996. *Evolutionary economics and the new international political economy.* London: Pinter.

Department of Regional Economic Expansion. 1986, 21 February. 'Federal and provincial regional development ministers meet.' News release.
- 1986, 29 October. 'Federal, provincial governments to encourage interprovincial trade.' News release.

Dewees, Donald, ed. 1983. *The regulation of quality.* Toronto: Butterworths.

Doern, G. Bruce. 1990. Industry, Science and Technology Canada: Is there industrial policy after free trade? In *How Ottawa Spends: 1990–91*, ed. Katherine Graham, 49–72. Ottawa: Carleton University Press.
- 1991. *Europe uniting: The EC model and Canada's constitutional debate.* Toronto: C.D. Howe Institute.
- 1996. Looking for the core: Industry Canada and program review. In *How Ottawa spends, 1996–97*, ed. Gene Swimmer, 73–98. Ottawa: Carleton University Press.
- 1995a. *Fairer play: Canadian competition policy institutions in a global market.* Toronto: C.D. Howe Institute.

– 1995b. The formation of Natural Resources Canada: New synergies or old departmental fiefdoms? Paper presented to the Workshop on the 1993 Federal Reorganization, Canadian Centre for Management Development.

Doern, G. Bruce, and Tom Conway. 1994. *The greening of Canada: Federal institutions and decisions.* Toronto: University of Toronto Press.

Doern, G. Bruce, and M. MacDonald. 1997. The Liberals' Internal Trade Agreement: The beginnings of a new federal assertiveness? In *How Ottawa Spends, 1997–98: Seeing red,* ed. Gene Swimmer, 135–58. Ottawa: Carleton University Press.

Doern, G. Bruce, Les Pal, and Brian Tomlin, eds. 1996. *Border crossings: The internationalization of Canadian public policy.* Toronto: Oxford University Press.

Doern, G. Bruce, and Brian Tomlin. 1991a. *Faith and fear: The Free Trade story.* Toronto: Stoddart.

– 1991b. The Free Trade sequel: Canada–United States subsidy negotiations. In *How Ottawa Spends: 1991–92,* ed. Frances Abele, 157–82. Ottawa, Carlton University Press.

– 1996. The internationalization of Canadian trade-industrial policy' In *Border crossings: The internationalization of Canadian public policy,* ed. G. Bruce Doern, Les Pal, and Brian Tomlin, 147–87. Toronto: Oxford University Press.

Doern, G. Bruce, and Glen Toner. 1985. *The politics of energy.* Toronto: Methuen.

Doern, G. Bruce, and Stephen Wilks, eds. 1996. *Comparative competition policy: National institutions in a global market.* Oxford: Clarendon Press.

Drache, Daniel, and M.S. Gertler, eds. 1991. *The new era of global competition.* Montreal: McGill-Queen's University Press.

Drushka, Ken. 1985. *Stumpted: The forestry industry in transition* Vancouver: Douglas & McIntyre.

Dunn, Christopher, ed. 1996. *Provinces: Canadian provincial politics.* Peterborough, ON: Broadview.

Eden, Lorraine, and Maureen Molot. 1993. Canada's national policies: Reflections on 125 years. *Canadian Public Policy* 19/3 (September): 232–60.

Esty, Daniel C. 1994. *Greening the GATT.* Washington, DC: Institute for International Economics.

Federal–Provincial Agricultural Trade Policy Committee. 1988. *Interprovincial barriers to trade in agriculture and food products.* Ottawa: Agriculture Canada.

Feltham, Ivan R., ed. 1996. *International trade dispute settlement: Implications for Canadian administrative law.* Ottawa: Centre for Trade Policy and Law.

Gagnon, Alain-G., ed. 1993. *Quebec: State and society,* 2d ed. Toronto: Nelson.

Gestrin, Michael, and Alan M. Rugman. 1993. *The NAFTA's impact on the North American investment regime.* Toronto: C.D. Howe Institute.

Gilson, J.C. 1989. *World agricultural changes: Implications for Canada.* Toronto: C.D. Howe Institute.

Haack, R.E., D.R. Hughes, and R.G. Shapiro. 1981. *The splintered market: Barriers to trade in Canadian agriculture.* Ottawa: Canadian Institute for Economic Policy.

Hadfield, Gillian, Robert Howse, and Michael Trebilcock. 1996, 28 August. *Rethinking consumer protection policy.* Paper presented to the University of Toronto Roundtable on New Approaches to Consumer Law. University of Toronto.

Hardin, Herschel. 1974. *A nation unaware: The Canadian economic culture.* Vancouver: J.J. Douglas.

Harris, Richard. 1993. *Trade, money and wealth in the Canadian economy.* Toronto: C.D. Howe Institute.

Harrison, Kathryn. 1994. Prospects for Harmonization in Environmental Policy. In *Canada: The State of the Federation, 1994,* ed. Douglas Brown and Janet Hiebert, 179–99. Kingston: Institute for Intergovernmental Relations.

– 1996. *Passing the buck: Federalism and Canadian environmental policy.* Vancouver: UBC Press.

Hart, Michael. 1993. The end of trade policy? In *Canada among nations: 1993–94,* ed. Fen Hampson and Christopher Maule, 85–105. Ottawa: Carleton University Press.

– *Decision at midnight.* Vancouver: UBC Press.

Harvey, David R. 1980. *Christmas turkey or prairie vulture? An economic analysis of the Crow's Nest Pass Grain Rates.* Montreal: Institute for Research on Public Policy.

Hoberg, G. 1997. North American environmental regulation.' In *Regulatory institutions in Britain and North America: Politics and paths to reform,* ed. G. Bruce Doern and Stephen Wilks, Toronto: University of Toronto Press.

Hoekman, Bernard, and Michel Kostecki. 1995. *The political economy of the world trading system.* Oxford: Oxford University Press.

Howse, Robert. 1995a. Between anarchy and the rule of law: Dispute settlement and related implementation issues in the Agreement on Internal Trade. In *Getting there,* ed. Michael Trebilcock and Daniel Schwanen, 170–95. Toronto: C.D. Howe Institute.

– 1995b. Economics, nationalism and reason: The limits of economic argument in the case against Quebec secession. *Canadian Business Law Journal* 25/2 (July): 305–25.

– 1996. Securing the Canadian Economic Union: Legal and constitutional options for the federal government. In *C.D. Howe Institute Commentary* no. 81. Toronto: C.D. Howe Institute.

Howse, Robert, and G. Heckman. 1996. The regulation of trade in electricity: A Canadian perspective. In *Ontario Hydro at the Millennium,* ed. R.J. Daniels, 105–55. Montreal: McGill-Queen's University Press.

Industry Canada. 1994. *Building a more innovative economy.* Ottawa: Minister of Supply and Services.

Industry, Science and Technology Canada. 1987, 27 November. 'Annual Conference of First Ministers: Barriers to interprovincial trade.' Document 800-24/060.

Interim Secretariat. 1992, 17 December. *Comprehensive negotiations on the Canadian internal market.* Discussion paper prepared by Interim Secretariat (later Internal Trade Secretariat). Ottawa: Industry Science and Technology Canada.

Internal Trade Secretariat. 1994. *Brief history of efforts to enhance internal trade in Canada.* Ottawa: Internal Trade Secretariat, Industry Canada.

Investment Canada. 1991. *A multinational investment accord: Issues, models and options.* Ottawa: Investment Canada.

Jacobs, S.H. 1995. Regulatory cooperation for an interdependent world: Issues for government' in OECD. In *Regulatory cooperation for an interdependent world,* 1–17. Paris: OECD.

Krugman, Paul R., and Maurice Obstfeld. 1994. *International economics: Theory and policy,* 3d ed. New York: HarperCollins.

Laplante, Benoit. 1990. Environmental regulation: Performance and design standards. In *Getting it green,* ed. Bruce Doern, 59–88. Toronto: C.D. Howe Institute.

LaSelva, Samuel V. 1993. Federalism as a way of life: Reflections on the Canadian experiment. *Canadian Journal of Political Science* 26/2 (June): 219–34.

Laux, Jeanne Kirk, and Maureen Molot. 1988. *State capitalism: Public enterprise in Canada.* Ithaca, NY: Cornell University Press.

Lenihan, Donald G. 1995. When a legitimate objective hits an unnecessary obstacle: Harmonizing regulations and standards in the Agreement on Internal Trade. In *Getting there,* ed. Michael J. Trebilcock and Daniel Schwanen, 98–118. Toronto: C.D. Howe Institute.

Leslie, P.M., K. Norrie, and I.K. Ip, eds. 1993. *A partnership in trouble: Renegotiating fiscal federalism.* Toronto: C.D. Howe Institute.

Leslie, P.M., and R.L. Watts, eds. 1988. *Canada: The state of the federation 1987–88.* Kingston: Institute of Intergovernmental Affairs.

Loizides, S., and M. Grant. 1992. *Barriers to interprovincial trade: Fifty case studies.* Ottawa: Conference Board of Canada.

Lustig, Michael. 1994. Constitutional paralysis: Why Canadian constitutional initiatives are doomed to fail. *Canadian Journal of Political Science* 27/4 (December): 747–72.

McDougall, John N. 1982. *Fuels and the national policy.* Toronto: Butterworths.

– 1986. Natural resources and national politics: A look at three Canadian resource industries. In *The politics of economic policy,* ed. Bruce Doern, 163–220. Toronto: University of Toronto Press.

McFetridge, Donald G. 1985. The economics of industrial policy: An overview. In *Canadian industrial policy in action*, ed. Donald McFetridge, 1–48. Toronto: University of Toronto Press.

– 1990. The economic approach to environmental issues. In *The environmental imperatives, getting it green*, ed. G. Bruce Doern, 84–169. Toronto: C.D. Howe Institute.

McGee, R. Harley. 1992. *Getting it right: Regional development in Canada.* Montreal: McGill-Queen's University Press.

McRoberts, K. 1985. Unilateralism, bilateralism and multilateralism: Approaches to Canadian federalism. In *Intergovernmental relations*, ed. R. Simeon, 71–130. Toronto: University of Toronto Press.

– 1993. Federal structures and the policy process. In *Governing Canada: Institutions and public policy*, ed. M.M. Atkinson. Toronto: Harcourt Brace Jovanovich.

McRoberts, K., and Patrick Monahan, eds. 1993. *The Charlottetown Accord, the referendum and the future of Canada.* Toronto: University of Toronto Press.

Menzie, E.L. 1988. Harmonization of farm policy for free interprovincial trade. *Canadian Journal of Agricultural Economics*, 36/4, Part I: 649–63.

Messinger, H. 1993. Interprovincial trade flows of goods and services. *Canadian Economic Observer*, Cat. 11–011, October.

Michael, Douglas C. 1996. Cooperative implementation of federal regulations. *Yale Journal on Regulation* 13/2 (Summer): 535–602.

Miller, Irving. 1995. Dispute resolution: An interprovincial approach. In *Getting there*, eds. Michael Trebilcock and Daniel Schwanen, 151–69. Toronto: C.D. Howe Institute.

Monohan, Patrick J. 1995. To the extent possible: A comment on dispute settlement in the Agreement on Internal Trade. In *Getting there*, ed. Michael Trebilcock and Daniel Schwanen, 211–18. Toronto: C.D. Howe Institute.

Morrow, J.D. 1994. *Game theory for political scientists.* Princeton, NJ: Princeton University Press.

Natural Resources Canada. 1993, 14 July. *Department of Natural Resources: Proposals for organizational structure.* Ottawa: Natural Resources Canada.

– 1994. *The state of Canada's forests.* Ottawa: Minister of Supply and Services

Nelles, H.V. 1974. *The politics of development: Forests, mines and hydro-electric power in Ontario.* Toronto: Macmillan.

Norrie, K., R. Simeon, and M. Krasnick. 1986. *Federalism and economic union in Canada.* Toronto: University of Toronto Press.

Oakley, Alan. 1990. *The challenge of free trade.* London: Harvester Wheatsheaf.

O'Brien, Robert. 1995. North American integration and international relations theory. *Canadian Journal of Political Science* 28/4 (December): 693–724.

OECD. 1990. Industrial subsidies in the OECD economies. *OECD Economic Studies*, no. 15. Paris: OECD.

– 1991. *The OECD declaration and decisions on international investment and multinational enterprises.* Paris: OECD.

Ontario. 1991. *Interprovincial trade barriers.* Toronto: Ontario Legislature Research Services.

Ostry, Sylvia. 1990. *Governments and corporations in a shrinking world: Trade and innovation policies in the United States, Europe and Japan.* New York: Council on Foreign Relations.

– 1993, 8–9 January. Globalization, domestic policies and the need for harmonization. Paper presented to Workshop on Competition Policy in a Global Economy, University of California.

Painter, Martin. 1991. Intergovernmental relations in Canada: An institutional analysis. *Canadian Journal of Political Science* 24/2 (June): 269–88.

Pal, Leslie A. 1997. *Beyond policy analysis.* Toronto: Nelson.

Palda, F. 1994. *Provincial trade wars: Why the blockade must end.* Vancouver: Fraser Institute.

Paquet, Gilles, and Jeffrey Roy. 1995. Prosperity through networks: The bottom-up strategy that might have been' In *How Ottawa Spends: 1995–96*, ed. Susan Phillips, 137–58. Ottawa: Carleton University Press.

Parsons, Graham F., and Peter Arcus. 1996. *Interprovincial trade and Canadian unity.* Calgary: Canada West Foundation.

Phidd, Richard W., and G. Bruce Doern. 1978. *The politics and management of Canadian economic policy.* Toronto: Macmillan.

Phillips, S.D. 1995. The Canada Health and Social Transfer: Fiscal federalism in search of a vision. In *Canada: The State of the Federation, 1995*, ed. D.M. Brown and J.W. Rose, 65–96. Kingston: Institute of Intergovernmental Relations.

Policy Research Committee. 1996, 4 October. *Growth, human development and social cohesion.* Ottawa: Unpublished draft interim report prepared for the Government of Canada.

Porter, Michael. 1990. *The competitive advantage of nations.* New York: Free Press.

– 1991. *Canada at the crossroads.* Ottawa: Business Council on National Issues and Government of Canada.

Premiers' Conference. 1986, 12 August. '27th annual Premiers' Conference, Communiqué on trade.' News release.

Prentice, Barry E. 1994. *Interprovincial barriers to agricultural trade.* Vancouver: Fraser Institute.

Prince, Michael. 1990. Little help on the prairie: Canadian farm income programs and the Western grain economy. In *How Ottawa Spends: 1990–91*, ed. Katherine Graham, 137–71. Ottawa: Carleton University Press.

Protheroe, David R. 1980. *Imports and politics.* Montreal: Institute for Research on Public Policy.

Purvis, D.D., and A. Raynauld. 1992. Lament for the Canadian economic union. In *Canada: The State of the Federation, 1992,* ed. D.M. Brown and R. Young, 129–43. Kingston: Institute of Intergovernmental Relations.

Quebec. Commission on the Political and Constitutional Future of Quebec. 199. *Final report.* Quebec City: Government of Quebec.

Quebec Liberal Party. Constitutional Committee. 1991. *A Quebec free to choose* [Allaire Report]. Quebec City: Quebec Liberal Party.

Raiffa, H. 1982. *The art and science of negotiation,* Cambridge, MA: Harvard University Press.

Rapoport, A., and A.M. Chammah. 1965. *Prisoner's dilemma: A study in conflict and cooperation,* Ann Arbor: University of Michigan Press.

Richards, John, and L. Pratt. 1979. *Prairie capitalism.* Toronto: McClelland & Stewart.

Robinson, Ian. 1993. The NAFTA, democracy and continental economic integration: Trade policy as if democracy mattered. In *How Ottawa spends: 1993–94,* ed. Susan Phillips, 333–81. Ottawa: Carleton University Press.

– 1995. Trade policy, globalization and the future of Canadian federalism. In *New trends in Canadian federalism,* ed. François Rocher and Miriam Smith, 270–87. Peterborough, ON: Broadview.

Rocher, François, and Miriam Smith. 1995. *New trends in Canadian federalism.* Peterborough, ON: Broadview.

Roy, Jeffrey. 1995. Understanding governance in high-technology regions: Towards a new paradigm of high technology and local development in Canada.' Unpublished paper, School of Public Administration, Carleton University, Ottawa.

Russell, Peter H. 1993. *Constitutional odyssey.* Toronto: University of Toronto Press.

Safarian, A.E. 1980. *Ten markets or one?* Toronto: Ontario Economic Council.

– 1993. *Multinational enterprise and public policy: A study of industrial countries.* Aldershot: Edward Elgar.

Saunders, J. Owen, ed. 1986. *Managing natural resources in a federal state.* Toronto: Carswell.

Savoie, Donald. 1986. *Regional economic development: Canada's search for solutions.* Toronto: University of Toronto Press.

– 1990. *The politics of public spending in Canada.* Toronto: University of Toronto Press.

Schultz, R.J. 1980. *Federalism, bureaucracy and public policy.* Montreal: McGill-Queen's University Press.

Schwanen, Daniel. 1995. Overview and key policy issues. In *Getting there*, ed. Michael Trebilcock and Daniel Schwanen, 1–19. Toronto: C.D. Howe Institute.

Schwartz, B. 1995. Assessing the Agreement on Internal Trade: The case for a 'More Perfect Union.' In *Canada: The State of the Federation, 1995*, ed. D.M. Brown and J.W. Rose. Kingston: Institute of Intergovernmental Relations.

Scott, Anthony, ed. 1976. *Natural resource revenues: A test of federalism*. Vancouver: University of British Columbia Press.

Shoyama, T.K. 1988. The Federal–provincial social contract. In *Canada: The state of the federation, 1987–88*, ed. Peter Leslie and Ronald Watts, 159–66. Kingston: Institute of Intergovernmental Relations.

Simeon, R. 1972. *Federal–provincial diplomacy*. Toronto: University of Toronto Press.

– 1990. Why did the Meech Lake Accord fail? In *Canada: The state of the federation, 1990*, ed. R.L. Watts and D.W. Brown, 15–40. Kingston: Institute of Intergovernmental Relations.

Sinclair, Scott. 1994. *Shifting powers, depressing standards: An analysis of the Internal Trade Agreement*. Ottawa: Canadian Centre for Policy Alternatives.

Skogstad, Grace. 1987. *The politics of agricultural policy making in Canada*. Toronto: University of Toronto Press.

– 1990a. The farm policy community in Ontario and Quebec. In *Policy communities and public policy in Canada*, ed. William D. Coleman and Grace Skogstad, 59–90. Toronto: Copp Clark Pitman.

– 1990b. The political economy of agriculture in Canada. In *The Political Economy of Agricultural Trade and Policy*, ed. H.J. Michelmann, J.C. Stabler, and G.G. Storey. Boulder, CO: Westview.

– 1992. The state, organized interests and Canadian agricultural trade policy: The impact of institutions. *Canadian Journal of Political Science* 25/2:319–47.

– 1993. Policy under siege: Supply management in agricultural marketing. *Canadian Public Administration*. 36/1 : 1–23.

– 1994. Agricultural trade and the international political economy. In *Political Economy and the Changing Global Order*, ed. R. Stubbs and G.R.D. Underhill. Toronto: McClelland & Stewart.

– 1995a. International trade agreements and Canadian supply management: Can the systems survive and adjust? In *Regulation and protectionism under GATT and NAFTA: Case studies in North American agriculture*, ed. G. Coffin, A. Schmitz, and K. Rosaasen. Boulder, CO: Westview.

– 1995b. Warring over wheat: Managing bilateral trading tensions. In *How Ottawa Spends, 1995–96*, ed. S.D. Phillips, 323–48. Ottawa: Carleton University Press.

– 1996. Agricultural Policy. In *Border crossings: The internationalization of Canadian public policy*, ed. Bruce Doern, Les Pal, and Brian Tomlin, 143–64. Toronto: Oxford University Press.

Slayton, Phillip, and Michael J. Trebilcock, ed. 1978. *The professions and public policy*. Toronto: University of Toronto Press.

Smiley, Donald. 1980. *Canada in question: Federalism in the eighties.* 3d ed. Toronto: McGraw-Hill Ryerson.

Smythe, Elizabeth. 1996. Capital mobility and the internationalization of Canadian investment policy. In *Border crossings: The internationalization of Canadian public policy*, ed. Bruce Doern, Leslie Pal, and Brian Tomlin, 186–206. Toronto: Oxford University Press.

Statistics Canada. 1996. *The economic benefits of interprovincial trade in Canada.* Ottawa: Statistics Canada

Stein, M.B. 1989. *Canadian constitutional renewal, 1968–1981: A case study in integrative bargaining.* Kingston: Institute of Intergovernmental Relations.

Stone, F. 1984. *Canada, the GATT and the international trade system.* Montreal: Institute for Research on Public Policy.

Swimmer, Gene, ed. 1996. *How Ottawa spends, 1996–97: Life under the knife.* Ottawa: Carleton University Press.

– 1997. *How Ottawa spends, 1997–98: Seeing red.* Ottawa: Carleton University Press.

Swinton, Katherine. 1995a. Courting our way to economic integration: Judicial review and the Canadian Economic Union. *Canadian Business Law Journal* 25/2 (July): 280–304.

– 1995b. Law, politics and the enforcement of the Agreement on Internal Trade. In *Getting there*, ed. Michael Trebilcock and Daniel Schwanen, 196–210. Toronto: C.D. Howe Institute.

Toner, Glen. 1986. Stardust: The tory energy program. In *How Ottawa spends: 1986–87*, ed. Michael J. Prince, 119–38. Toronto: Methuen.

– 1995. The green plan: From great expectations to eco-backtracking ... to revitalization? In *How Ottawa spends, 1994–95*, ed. S.D. Phillips, 225–60. Ottawa: Carleton University Press.

Trebilcock, Michael J. 1983a. Regulating service quality in professional markets. In *The regulation of quality*, ed. Donald Dewees, 83–108. Toronto: Butterworths.

Trebilcock, Michael J., ed. 1983b. *Federalism and the Economic Union.* Toronto: Ontario Economic Council.

Trebilcock, Michael J., and Rambod Behboodi. 1995. The Canadian Agreement on Internal Trade: Retrospect and prospects. In *Getting there*, ed. Michael J. Trebilcock and Daniel Schwanen, 20–89. Toronto: C.D. Howe Institute.

Trebilcock, Michael J., and Robert W. Howse. 1995. *The regulation of international trade.* London: Routledge.

Trebilcock, Michael J., and Daniel Schwanen, eds. 1995. *Getting there: An assessment of the Agreement on Internal Trade.* Toronto: C.D. Howe Institute.

Trent, John E., Robert Young, and Guy Lachapelle, eds. 1996. *Quebec–Canada: What is the path ahead?* Ottawa: University of Ottawa Press.

Tupper, Allan. 1986. Federalism and the politics of industrial policy. In *Industrial policy*, ed. Andre Blais, 347–78. Toronto: University of Toronto Press.

Tupper, Allan, and G. Bruce Doern, eds. 1981. *Public corporations and public policy in Canada.* Montreal: Institute for Research on Public Policy.

– 1988. *Privatization, public policy and public corporations in Canada.* Montreal: Institute for Research on Public Policy.

Vollans, Garry E. 1995. The decline of natural monopolies in the energy sector. *Energy Studies Review,* 7/3: 247–61.

Wade, Robert. 1990. *Governing the market.* Princeton, NJ: Princeton University Press.

Watts, R.L. 1989a. *Executive federalism: A comparative analysis.* Kingston: Institute of Intergovernmental Relations.

– 1989b. An overview. In *Canada: The State of the Federation, 1989*, ed. R.L. Watts and D.W. Brown, 3–19. Kingston: Institute of Intergovernmental Relations.

Watts, Ronald, and Douglas M. Brown, eds. 1991. *Options for a new Canada.* Toronto: University of Toronto Press.

Whittington, M., and R. Van Loon. 1996. *Canadian government and politics: Institutions and processes.* Toronto: McGraw-Hill Ryerson.

Williams, Allan M. 1991. *The European Community.* Oxford: Blackwell.

Williams, Glen. 1983. *Not for export.* Toronto: McClelland & Stewart.

Wolfe, David. 1993, 6 June. The wealth of regions: Rethinking industrial policy. Paper presented to the Canadian Political Science Association, Carleton University, Ottawa.

Woodside, Kenneth B. 1993. Trade and industrial policy: Hard choices. In *Governing Canada: Institutions and public policy*, ed. Michael Atkinson, 241–74. Toronto: Harcourt Brace.

Young, H.P. 1991. *Negotiation Analysis.* Ann Arbor: University of Michigan Press.

Young, R., and D.M. Brown. 1992. Overview. In *Canada: The state of the federation, 1992*, ed. D.M. Brown and R. Young, 3–24. Kingston: Institute of Intergovernmental Relations.

Index

Agreement on Internal Trade (AIT),
4, 7, 9–13, 17, 20, 34–5, 37, 52,
151–2; administrative structure,
44–5; constitutional links, 38–9; dispute-resolution, 12–13, 137–40,
161–3 (*see also* dispute resolution);
federal government strategy, 21;
and federalism, 31; federal trade-
and-commerce power, 146–9, 161;
framework principles and applications, 46–7; future of, 163–8; general rules, 10–11, 104, 134–7, 155;
harmonization, 136; horizontal
chapters, 9; institutional development, 43–6; institutional provisions,
12, 44–5, 51, 53–6, 137–40; legitimate objectives, 11, 155 (*see also*
legitimate objectives); multi-policy
negotiations, 17–18, 26, 81, 116–18,
154, 158–61; negotiating process,
12, 31–2, 45–6, 47–8, 154–8; negotiating stages, 37, 48–53, 155; negotiating strategies, 7, 50; negotiations,
25, 135–6, 140–2; performance
standards, 136–7, 149; response to,
152–3; specific rules, 10
agriculture and food goods chapter

(AIT), 121–7, 158; barriers to,
124–5; and federal–provincial agricultural policy, 122; provincial
stance(s), 124; supply management, 121, 123; and trade policy,
122–3, 126
Alberta, role in AIT, 7, 60–2, 81, 155–6
Atlantic provinces, role in AIT, 12,
73–8, 82, 156

Breton, Albert, 30
British Columbia, role in AIT, 7–8,
68–70, 81, 156

Canada Assistance Plan, 34
Canada Health and Social Transfer,
34, 93
Canadian Centre for Policy Alterna-
tives, 153
Canadian Chamber of Commerce, 152
Canadian Council of Ministers of the
Environment (CCME), 111–12, 116
Canadian International Development
Agency, 86
Canadian Labour Force Development
Board, 106
capitalist system frictions, 23

capital mobility, 100–1, 102–3
Charlottetown Accord, 8, 17, 28, 38, 66, 105; and social charter, 33
chief negotiators, 54, 95–6, 102
Chrétien government, 33
Chrétien, Jean, 37, 39
Clark, Glen, 69
Code of Economic Conduct, 40
Committee of Ministers on Internal Trade (CMIT), 43–6, 51–2, 53–4, 105
Committee of Regional Economic Development Ministers (CREDM), 41
Committee on Internal Trade, 12
comparative advantage (theory), 5
constitution (Canada), 8, 11, 38
constitutional policy, 27

Department of External Affairs, 19
Department of Foreign Affairs and International Trade (DFAIT), 24
Department of Industry, Trade and Commerce, 19
Department of Regional Economic Expansion (DREE), 19
Department of Regional Industrial Expansion (DRIE), 19
dispute-resolution procedures (of AIT), 12–13, 59, 137–40, 149; and federal trade-and-commerce power, 146–9; UPS case, 142–6
Downey, Jim, 63

economic development policy (Canada), 7, 8, 19, 41–2; *see also* regional economic development economic union
elite accommodation, 26, 28
energy in AIT, 130–2, 158; electricity, 131–2; federal stance, 131; provincial stance(s), 131–2
environmental non-governmental organizations (ENGOs), 111, 115–16, 118
environment chapter (AIT), 110–16, 157; federal stance, 115; provincial stance(s), 112–13, 115; regulation policy, 113–14; sustainable development, 114; trade context, 110–11, 112
Established Program Financing, 34
Europe, 3
European Union (EU), 6, 25, 33
executive federalism, 26–7

federal government, 81, 101–2, 155–6
federalism, 3, 5–6, 26; bilateral versus multilateral, 26–7; and decision making, 26–7; and game theory, 30–1; as Prisoner's Dilemma, 30; and social policy, 32–5
Federal–Provincial Agricultural Trade Policy Committee (FPATPC), 123–4
federal–provincial policy (Canada), 17, 26–32, 45
federal–provincial relations (Canada), 4, 111, 154; and trade policy, 29–30
federal spending power, 34; trade-and-commerce power, 146–9
First Ministers, 53
Forum of Labour Market Ministers (FLMM), 105
free trade, 3, 5, 21–2; and federalism, 4–9
Free Trade Agreement (FTA), 3, 21, 24–5, 29–30
free-trade federalism (Canada), 3, 4, 6–7, 135, 152, 163–5; historical context, 17; and national unity, 8–9